WEBSTER'S

COMPACT

WRITERS GUIDE

Webster's
COMPACT
WRITERS
GUIDE

A Merriam-Webster®

MERRIAM-WEBSTER INC.

Springfield, Massachusetts

Copyright © 1987 by Merriam-Webster Inc.

Philippines Copyright 1987 by Merriam-Webster Inc.

Library of Congress Cataloging in Publication
Main entry under title:

Webster's compact writers guide.

   1. Authorship—Style—Handbooks, manuals, etc.
I. Merriam-Webster, Inc.
PE1421.W38   1987   808'.02   86-28650
ISBN 0-87779-187-2

CONTENTS

PREFACE

Webster's Compact Writers Guide is designed to be a concise guide to the basic conventions of English in its written form. Writers and editors generally use the word *style* to refer to these conventions, which include such matters as punctuating sentences, capitalizing names and terms, using italics or underlining, and deciding when to use abbreviations and numerals.

This book offers information and advice across this entire range of topics as well as information about writing and styling bibliographical references. For each topic, the book offers concise and comprehensive descriptions of the rules and conventions that writers and editors have developed for themselves to help them prepare copy that is clear, consistent, and attractive. Where the rules and conventions have exceptions, variations, and fine points that readers need to know about, these are also presented.

In many cases, the styling conventions discussed in this book offer choices rather than a single rule, as over the years writers and editors have developed differing sets of rules to guide them in matters of style. One writer may favor a particular way of deciding when to use numerals and when to spell out numbers or how to form possessives of proper nouns ending in *s,* while another writer may favor other ways. Neither of these writers is necessarily wrong; each may simply be following a different style.

There are, of course, limits on the range of acceptable style available to writers. And within that acceptable range, most writers and editors try to be consistent in the choices they make regarding matters of style. Style books are designed to help writers and editors in their job of making acceptable and consistent styling choices.

Like most other style books, *Websters Compact Writers Guide* was written and edited by working editors, the editors at Merriam-Webster Inc., and it reflects their experience in writing and editing for publication. However, the styling conventions described in this book are by no means meant to be exhaustive of or limited to the style rules followed in Merriam-Webster® publications. Instead, this manual is based on Merriam-Webster's continuous study of the ways that Americans use their language. It draws on our extensive citation files, which include more than 13 million examples of English words used in context, gathered from books by respected authors, major metropolitan newspapers, widely circulated general-interest magazines, and other publications, such as newsletters, annual reports, and special mailings by corporations and other institutions. Working from these sources, Merriam-Webster editors have been able to establish which styling conventions are most commonly followed in standard American prose.

Based as it is on this kind of study, the book offers readers information about both the consensus and the variety that are apparent in standard American style. The consensus in this book is recorded with simple descriptive statements, such as "A period terminates a sentence or a sentence fragment that is neither interrogative nor exclamatory."

In some cases, these statements have to be qualified, as in "The abbreviations A.D. and B.C. are usually styled in typeset matter as punctuated, unspaced, small capitals. . . ." The term *usually* is used throughout this manual to indicate that we have evidence that some writers and editors follow a different styling practice from the one that we are describing. However, *usually* appears only in statements describing a styling practice that is clearly the prevalent practice. Hence, the writer who prefers AD or A.D. or AD knows that he or she is departing from the prevalent practice but that such departures are not unprecedented in standard style.

In describing styling practices that are clearly not prevalent, we have used the word *sometimes* to qualify the descriptive statement, as in "Commas are sometimes used to separate main clauses that are not joined by conjunctions." In most cases, a descriptive statement qualified with *sometimes* is also accompanied by an additional explanation that tells the reader what the circumstances are under which the styling is most likely to occur and what the common alternatives to this styling are. In the case of the example just cited, the reader is told that this styling is likely to be used if the main clauses are short and feature obvious parallelism. The reader is also told that using a comma to join clauses that are not short or obviously parallel is usually considered an error, that most writers avoid it, and that clauses not joined by conjunctions are usually separated with a semicolon.

The qualifiers *often* and *frequently* are used throughout the manual without meaning to suggest anything about the prevalence of the styling practice being described except that it is not universally followed. We say, for instance, that "a comma is often used to set off the word *Incorporated* or the abbreviation *Inc.* from the rest of a corporate name; however, many companies elect to omit this comma from their names." In saying this, we are not trying to say whether most companies do or do not favor using a comma in this position. We are saying that both practices are so well-established within standard style that their relative frequency is fundamentally irrelevant.

Finally, some styling practices raise questions demanding explanations that go beyond the use of a simple qualifier. In these cases, we have appended a note to the description. Notes are introduced by the all-capitalized designation "NOTE," and they serve to explain, in as much detail as needed, variations, exceptions, and fine points that relate to or qualify the descriptive statement that precedes them.

Webster's Compact Writers Guide is adapted from *Webster's Standard American Style Manual* and, as such, is based on the work done by the writers and editors of that book. The adaptation was carried out by Julie A. Collier, Associate Editor. The index for this book was prepared by Eileen M. Haraty, Assistant Editor. Manuscript typing was done by Helene Gingold, Department Secretary. Proofreading was done by Madeline L. Novak, Associate Editor; Daniel J. Hopkins, Assistant Editor; and Kelly L. Tierney, Editorial Assistant.

Chapter 1

Punctuation

CONTENTS

Punctuation marks are used in the English writing system to help clarify the structure and meaning of sentences. To some degree, they achieve this end by corresponding to certain elements of the spoken language, such as pitch, volume, pause, and stress. To an even greater degree, however, punctuation marks serve to clarify structure and meaning by virtue of the fact that they conventionally accompany certain grammatical elements in a sentence, no matter how those elements might be spoken. In many cases, the relationship between punctuation and grammatical structure is such that the choice of which mark of punctuation to use in a sentence is clear and unambiguous. In other cases, however, the structure of a sentence may be such that it allows for several patterns of punctuation. In cases like these, varying notions of correctness have grown up, and two writers might, with equal correctness and with equal clarity, punctuate the same sentence quite differently.

This chapter is designed to help writers and editors make decisions about which mark of punctuation to use. In situations where more than one pattern of punctuation may be used, each is explained; if there are reasons to prefer one over another, the reasons are presented. However, even after having read this chapter, writers and editors will find that they still encounter questions requiring them to exercise their judgment and taste.

The descriptions in this chapter focus on the ways in which punctuation marks are used to convey grammatical structure. The chapter does not explain in any detailed way the use of some punctuation marks to style individual words and compounds. Specifically, this chapter does not discuss the use of quotation marks to style titles and other kinds of proper nouns, the use of apostrophes to form plurals and possessives, the use of hyphens to form compounds, or the use of periods to punctuate abbreviations. For a discussion of these topics, see Chapter 2, "Capitals, Italics, and Quotation Marks"; Chapter 3, "Plurals, Possessives, and Compounds"; and Chapter 4, "Abbreviations."

General Principles

In addition to the rules that have been developed for individual marks of punctuation, there are also conventions and principles that apply to marks of punctuation in general, and these are explained in the paragraphs that follow.

Open and Close Punctuation

Two terms frequently used to describe patterns of punctuation, especially in regard to commas, are *open* and *close*. An open punctuation pattern is one in which commas and other marks of punctuation are used sparingly, usually only to separate major syntactical units, such as main clauses, or to prevent misreading. A close punctuation pattern, on the other hand, makes liberal use of punctuation marks, often putting one wherever the grammatical structure of the sentence will allow it. Close punctuation is often considered old-fashioned, and open punctuation more modern; however, contemporary writing displays a wide range of practices in regard to commas, and some grammatical constructions are still punctuated in ways traditionally associated with close punctuation (see paragraphs 8 and 22 under Comma in this chapter).

Multiple Punctuation

The term *multiple punctuation* describes the use of two or more marks of punctuation following the same word in a sentence. A conventional rule says that multiple punctuation is to be avoided except in cases involving brackets, parentheses, quotation marks, and sometimes dashes. Unfortunately, it is not possible to formulate any simple general instructions that would allow writers and editors to apply this rule. This book addresses the question of multiple punctuation by including a section entitled "With Other Marks of Punctuation" at the end of the treatment of each mark of punctuation for which there is a specific convention regarding multiple punctuation.

Boldface and Italic Punctuation

In general, marks of punctuation are set in the same typeface (lightface or boldface, italic or roman) as the word that precedes them, but most writers and editors allow themselves a number of exceptions to this rule. Brackets and parentheses are nearly always set in the font of the surrounding text, usually lightface roman, regardless of the text they enclose. Quotation marks are usually handled in the same manner; however, if the text they enclose is entirely in a contrasting typeface, they are set in a typeface to match. Some writers and editors base decisions regarding the typeface of exclamation points and question marks on the context in which they are used. If the exclamation point or question mark is clearly associated with the word or words that precede it, it is set in a matching typeface. If, on the other hand, it punctuates the sentence as a whole, it is set in the typeface of the sentence.

> **Summary:** Recently completed surveys confirm the theory that ...
>
> You did *that!*
>
> We were talking with the author of the book *Who Did That?*
>
> Have you seen the latest issue of *Saturday Review?*

Spacing

The conventions regarding the amount of space that precedes or follows a mark of punctuation vary from mark to mark. In general, the usual spacing around each mark of punctuation should be clear from the example sentences included for each mark of punctuation. In cases where additional explanation is needed, it is included at the end of the discussion, often under the heading "Spacing."

Ampersand

An ampersand is typically written &, although it has other forms, as *&*, *&*, and &. The character represents the word *and*; its function is to replace the word when a shorter form is desirable. However, the ampersand is an acceptable substitute for *and* only in a few constructions.

1. The ampersand is used in the names of companies but not in the names of agencies that are part of the federal government.

    > American Telephone & Telegraph Co.
    > Gulf & Western Corporation
    > Occupational Safety and Health Administration
    > Securities and Exchange Commission

    NOTE: In styling corporate names, writers and editors often try to reproduce the form of the name preferred by the company (taken from an annual report or company letterhead). However, this information may not be available and, even if it is available, following the different preferences of different companies can lead to apparent inconsistencies in the text. Publications that include very many corporate names usually choose one styling, usually the one with the ampersand, and use it in all corporate names that include *and*.

2. Ampersands are frequently used in abbreviations. Style varies regarding the spacing around the ampersand. Publications that make heavy use of abbreviations, such as business or technical publications, most often omit the spaces. In general-interest publications, both the spaced and the unspaced stylings are common.

    > The R&D budget looks adequate for the next fiscal year.
    > Apply for a loan at your bank or S & L.

3. The ampersand is often used in cases where a condensed text is necessary, as in tabular material. While bibliographies, indexes, and most other listings use *and*, some systems of parenthetical documentation do use the ampersand. For more on parenthetical documentation, see Chapter 6, "Notes and Bibliographies."

   (Carter, Good & Robertson 1984)

4. When an ampersand is used between the last two elements in a series, the comma is omitted.

   the law firm of Shilliday, Fraser & French

Apostrophe

1. The apostrophe is used to indicate the possessive case of nouns and indefinite pronouns. For details regarding this use, see the section on Possessives, beginning on page 150, in Chapter 3, "Plurals, Possessives, and Compounds."

2. Apostrophes are sometimes used to form plurals of letters, numerals, abbreviations, symbols, and words referred to as words. For details regarding this use, see the section on Plurals, beginning on page 140 in Chapter 3, "Plurals, Possessives, and Compounds."

3. Apostrophes mark omissions in contractions made of two or more words that are pronounced as one word.

> didn't
> you're
> o'clock
> shouldn't've

4. The apostrophe is used to indicate that letters have been intentionally omitted from the spelling of a word in order to reproduce a perceived pronunciation or to give a highly informal flavor to a piece of writing.

> "Head back to N'Orleans," the man said.
>
> Get 'em while they're hot.
>
> dancin' till three

NOTE: Sometimes words are so consistently spelled with an apostrophe that the spelling with the apostrophe becomes an accepted variant.

> fo'c'sle for *forecastle*
> bos'n for *boatswain*
> rock 'n' roll for *rock and roll*

5. Apostrophes mark the omission of numerals.

> class of '86
> politics in the '80s

NOTE: Writers who use the apostrophe for styling the plurals of words expressed in numerals usually avoid the use of the apostrophe illustrated in the second example above. Either they omit the apostrophe that stands for the missing figures, or they spell the word out.

> 80's   *or*   eighties   *but not*   '80's

6. Apostrophes are used to produce the inflected forms of verbs that are made of numerals or individually pronounced letters. Hyphens are sometimes used for this purpose also.

> 86'ed our proposal
> OK'ing the manuscript
> TKO'd his opponent

7. An apostrophe is often used to add an *-er* ending to an abbreviation, especially if some confusion might result from its absence. Hyphens are sometimes used for this purpose also. If no confusion is likely, the apostrophe is usually omitted.

> 4-H'er
> AA'er
> CBer
> DXer

8. The use of apostrophes to form abbreviations (as *ass'n* for *association* or *sec'y* for *secretary*) is avoided in most formal writing.

Brackets

Brackets work like parentheses to set off inserted material, but their functions are more specialized. Several of their principal uses occur with quoted material, as illustrated below. For other aspects of styling quotations, see Quotation Marks, Double, and Quotation Marks, Single, in this chapter.

With Editorial Insertions

1. Brackets enclose editorial comments, corrections, clarifications, or other material inserted into a text, especially into quoted matter.

> "Remember, this was the first time since it became law that the Twenty-first Amendment [outlining procedures for the replacement of a dead or incapacitated President or Vice President] had been invoked."

> "But there's one thing to be said for it [his apprenticeship with Samuels]: it started me thinking about architecture in a new way."

> He wrote, "I am just as cheerful as when you was [sic] here."

NOTE: While the text into which such editorial insertions are made is almost always quoted material, they are sometimes also used in nonquoted material, particularly in cases where an editor wishes to add material to an author's text without disturbing the author's original wording.

> Furthermore the Committee anticipates additional expenses in the coming fiscal year [October 1985–September 1986] and seeks revenues to meet these expenses.

2. Brackets set off insertions that supply missing letters.

"If you can't persuade D[israeli], I'm sure no one can."

3. **Brackets enclose insertions that take the place of words or phrases that were used in the original version of a quoted passage.**

> The report, entitled "A Decade of Progress," begins with a short message from President Stevens in which she notes that "the loving portraits and revealing accounts of [this report] are not intended to constitute a complete history of the decade. . . . Rather [they] impart the flavor of the events, developments, and achievements of this vibrant period."

4. **Brackets enclose insertions that slightly alter the form of a word used in an original text.**

> The magazine reported that thousands of the country's children were "go[ing] to bed hungry every night."

5. **Brackets are used to indicate that the capitalization or typeface of the original passage has been altered in some way.**

> As we point out on page 164, "The length of a quotation usually determines whether it is run into the text or set as a block quotation . . . . [L]ength can be assessed in terms of number of words, the number of typewritten or typeset lines, or the number of sentences in the passage."

> They agreed with and were encouraged by her next point: "In the past, many secretaries have been placed in positions of responsibility *without being delegated enough authority to carry out the responsibility*. [Italics

added.] The current pressures affecting managers have caused them to rethink the secretarial function and to delegate more responsibility and authority to their secretaries."

NOTE: In situations in which meticulous handling of original source material is required, a capital M in the example given above would be placed in brackets to indicate that it was not capitalized in the original source.

They agreed with and were encouraged by her next point: "[M]any secretaries have been placed in positions of responsibility without being delegated enough authority to carry out the responsibility."

As a Mechanical Device

6. Brackets function as parentheses within parentheses.

   The company was incinerating high concentrations of pollutants (such as polychlorinated biphenyls [PCBs]) in a power boiler.

7. Brackets set off phonetic symbols or transcriptions.

   [t] in British *duty*

8. Brackets are used in combination with parentheses (and occasionally braces) to indicate units contained within larger units in mathematical copy. They are also used in chemical formulas.

   $$x + 5[(x+y)(2x-y)]$$
   $$NH_4[Cr(NH_3)_2(SCN)_4] \cdot H_2O$$

With Other Marks of Punctuation

9. No punctuation mark (other than a period after an abbreviation) precedes bracketed material within a sentence. If punctuation is required, the mark is placed after the closing bracket.

   > The report stated, "If we fail to find additional sources of supply [of oil and gas], our long-term growth will be limited."

10. When brackets enclose a complete sentence, the required punctuation should be placed within the brackets.

    > [A paw print photographed last month in the Quabbin area has finally verified the cougar's continued existence in the Northeast.]

    NOTE: Unlike parentheses, brackets are rarely used to enclose complete sentences within other sentences.

Spacing

11. No space is left between brackets and the material they enclose or between brackets and any mark of punctuation immediately following.

12. In typewritten material, two spaces precede an opening bracket and follow a closing bracket when the brackets enclose a complete sentence. In typeset material, one space is used.

We welcome the return of the cougar. [A paw print photographed last month has verified its existence locally.] Its habitation in this area is a good sign for the whole environment.

We welcome the return of the cougar. [A paw print photographed last month has verified its existence locally.] Its habitation in this area is a good sign for the whole environment.

Colon

The colon is a mark of introduction. It indicates that what follows it—whether a clause, a phrase, or even a single word—is linked with some element that precedes it. Many uses of the colon are similar to those of the dash. Like the dash, the colon gives special emphasis to whatever follows it; lengthy material introduced by a colon is often further emphasized by indention. (For information on the question of capitalizing the first word following a colon, see the section on Beginnings, starting on page 92, in Chapter 2, "Capitals, Italics, and Quotation Marks.")

With Phrases and Clauses

1. A colon introduces a clause or phrase that explains, illustrates, amplifies, or restates what has gone before.

The sentence was poorly constructed: it lacked both unity and coherence.

Throughout its history, the organization has combined a tradition of excellence with a dedication to human service: educating the young, caring for the elderly, assisting in community-development programs.

Disk cartridges provide high-density storage capacity: up to 16 megabytes of information on some cartridges.

Time was running out: a decision had to be made.

2. A colon directs attention to an appositive.

The question is this: where will we get the money?

He had only one pleasure: eating.

3. A colon is used to introduce a series. The introductory statement often includes a phrase such as *the following* or *as follows*.

The conference was attended by representatives of five nations: England, France, Belgium, Spain, and Portugal.

Anyone planning to participate should be prepared to do the following: hike five miles with a backpack, sleep on the ground without a tent, and paddle a canoe through rough water.

NOTE: Opinion varies regarding whether a colon should interrupt the grammatical continuity of a clause (as by coming between a verb and its objects). Although most style manuals and composition handbooks advise against this practice and recommend that a full independent clause precede the colon, the interrupting colon is common. It is especially likely to be used before a lengthy and complex list, in which case the colon serves to set the list distinctly apart from the normal flow of running text. With shorter or less complex lists, the colon is usually not used.

> Our programs to increase profitability include: continued modernization of our manufacturing facilities; consolidation of distribution terminals; discontinuation of unprofitable retail outlets; and reorganization of our personnel structure, along with across-the-board staff reductions.

> Our programs to increase profitability include plant modernization, improved distribution and retailing procedures, and staff reductions.

> Our programs to increase profitability include the following: continued modernization of our manufacturing facilities; consolidation of distribution terminals; discontinuation of unprofitable retail outlets; and reorganization of our personnel structure, along with across-the-board staff reductions.

4. A colon is used like a dash to introduce a summary statement following a series.

> Physics, biology, sociology, anthropology: he discusses them all.

With Quotations

5. A colon introduces lengthy quoted material that is set off from the rest of a text by indentation but not by quotation marks.

> He took the title for his biography of Thoreau from a passage in *Walden*:

I long ago lost a hound, a bay horse, and a turtle-dove, and am still on their trail . . . . I have met one or two who had heard the hound, and the tramp of the horse, and even seen the dove disappear behind a cloud, and they seemed as anxious to recover them as if they had lost them themselves.

However, the title *A Hound, a Bay Horse, and a Turtle-Dove* probably puzzled some readers.

6. A colon may be used before a quotation in running text, especially when (1) the quotation is lengthy, (2) the quotation is a formal statement or is being given special emphasis, or (3) the quotation is an appositive.

Said Murdoch: "The key to the success of this project is good planning. We need to know precisely all of the steps that we will need to go through, what kind of staff we will require to accomplish each step, what the entire project will cost, and when we can expect completion."

The inscription reads: "Here lies one whose name was writ in water."

In response, he had this to say: "No one knows better than I do that changes will have to be made soon."

As a Mechanical Device

7. In transcriptions of dialogue, a colon follows the speaker's name.

Robert: You still haven't heard from her?
Michael: No, and I'm beginning to worry.

8. A colon follows a brief heading or introductory term.

> NOTE: The library will be closed on the 17th while repairs are being made to the heating system.
>
> 1977: New developments in microchip technology lead to less-expensive manufacturing.

9. A colon separates elements in page references, bibliographical and biblical citations, and fixed formulas used to express ratios and time.

> *Journal of the American Medical Association* 48:356
> Springfield, Mass.: Merriam-Webster Inc.
> John 4:10
> 8:30 a.m.
> a ratio of 3:5

10. A colon separates titles and subtitles (as of books).

> *The Tragic Dynasty: A History of the Romanovs*

11. A colon is used to join terms that are being contrasted or compared.

> Seventeenth-century rhymes include *prayer* : *afar* and *brass* : *was* : *ass.*

12. A colon follows the salutation in formal correspondence.

> Dear General Smith:
> Dear Product Manager:
> Dear Mr. Jiménez:
> Ladies and Gentlemen:

13. A colon punctuates memorandum and government correspondence headings and subject lines in general business letters.

          TO:
          VIA:
          SUBJECT:
          REFERENCE:

14. A colon separates writer/dictator/typist initials in the identification lines of business letters.

          WAL:jml
          WAL:WEB:jml

15. A colon separates carbon-copy or blind carbon-copy abbreviations from the initials or names of copy recipients in business letters.

          cc:RWP
            JES

          bcc:MWK
            FCM

With Other Marks of Punctuation

16. A colon is placed outside quotation marks and parentheses.

          There's only one thing wrong with "Harold's Indiscretion": it's not funny.

          I quote from the first edition of *Springtime in Savannah* (published in 1952):

Spacing

17. In typewritten material, two spaces follow a colon used in running text, bibliographical references, publication titles, and letter or memorandum headings. In typeset material, only one space follows.

> The answer is simple: don't go.
> SUBJECT: Project X
> New York: Macmillan, 1980.
> *Typewriting: A Guide*

18. When a colon is being used between two correlated terms (see paragraph 11), it is centered with equal spacing on each side.

> The stature apparent in the two sexes shows the same female : male proportions.

19. No space precedes or follows a colon when it is used between numerals.

> 9:30 a.m.
> a ratio of 2:4

20. No space precedes or follows a colon in a business-letter identification line or in a carbon-copy notation that indicates a recipient designated by initials.

> FCM:hg
> cc:FCM

21. Two spaces follow a colon in a carbon-copy notation that indicates a recipient designated by a full name.

> cc: Mr. Johnson

Comma

The comma is the most frequently used punctuation mark in the English writing system. Its most common uses are to separate items in a series and to set off syntactical elements within sentences. Within these two broad categories, there are a great many specific uses to which commas can be put. This section explains the most common aspects of the comma, listed under the following headings.

Between Main Clauses

1. A comma separates main clauses joined by a coordinating conjunction (as *and, but, or, nor,* and *for*). For use of commas with clauses joined by correlative conjunctions, see paragraph 24 below.

She knew very little about him, and he volunteered nothing.

We will not respond to any more questions on that topic this afternoon, nor will we respond to similar questions at any time in the future.

His face showed disappointment, for he knew that he had failed.

NOTE: Some reference books still insist that *so* and *yet* are adverbs rather than conjunctions and that therefore they should be preceded by a semicolon when they join main clauses. However, our evidence indicates that the use of *so* and *yet* as conjunctions preceded by a comma is standard.

The acoustics in this hall are good, so every note is clear.

We have requested this information many times before, yet we have never gotten a satisfactory reply.

2. When one or both of the clauses are short or when they are closely related in meaning, the comma is often omitted.

The sun was shining and the birds were singing.

We didn't realize it at the time but the spot we had picked for our home was the same spot one of our ancestors had picked for his home.

Six thousand years ago, the top of the volcano blew off in a series of powerful eruptions and the sides collapsed into the middle.

Many people want to take their vacations in August so it may be difficult for some of them to find good accommodations.

NOTE: In punctuating sentences such as the ones illustrated above, writers have to use their own judgment regarding whether clauses are short enough or closely related enough to warrant omitting the comma. There are no clear-cut rules to follow; however, factors such as the rhythm, parallelism, or logic of the sentence often influence how clearly or smoothly it will read with or without the comma.

3. Commas are sometimes used to separate main clauses that are not joined by conjunctions. This styling is especially likely to be used if the clauses are short and feature obvious parallelism.

> One day you are a successful corporate lawyer, the next day you are out of work.
> The city has suffered terribly in the interim. Bombs have destroyed most of the buildings, disease has ravaged the population.

NOTE: Using a comma to join clauses that are neither short nor obviously parallel is usually called *comma fault* or *comma splice* and most writers and editors avoid such a construction. In general, clauses not joined by conjunctions are separated by semicolons.

4. If a sentence is composed of three or more clauses, the clauses may be separated by either commas or semicolons. Clauses that are short and relatively free of commas can be separated by commas even if they are not joined by a conjunction. If the

clauses are long or heavily punctuated, they are separated with semicolons, except for the last two clauses which may be separated by either a comma or a semicolon. Usually a comma will be used between the last two clauses only if those clauses are joined by a conjunction. For more examples of clauses separated with commas and semicolons, see paragraph 5 under Semicolon in this chapter.

> The pace of change seems to have quickened, the economy is uncertain, the technology seems sometimes liberating and sometimes hostile.
>
> Small fish fed among the marsh weed, ducks paddled along the surface, and a muskrat ate greens along the bank.
>
> The policy is a complex one to explain; defending it against its critics is not easy, nor is it clear the defense is always necessary.

With Compound Predicates

5. Commas are not usually used to separate the parts of a compound predicate.

> The firefighter tried to enter the burning building but was turned back by the thick smoke.

NOTE: Despite the fact that most style manuals and composition handbooks warn against separating the parts of compound predicates with commas, many authors and editors use commas in just this way. They are particularly likely to do so if the predicate is especially long and complicated, if they want to stress one part of the predicate, or if the absence of a comma could cause even a momentary misreading of the sentence.

> The board helps to develop the financing, new product planning, and marketing strategies for new corporate divisions, and issues periodic reports on expenditures, revenues, and personnel appointments.
>
> This is an unworkable plan, and has been from the start.
>
> I try to explain to him what I want him to do, and get nowhere.

With Subordinate Clauses and Phrases

6. Adverbial clauses and phrases that precede a main clause are usually set off with commas.

> As cars age, they depreciate.
>
> Having made that decision, we turned our attention to other matters.
>
> To understand the situation, you must be familiar with the background.
>
> From the top of this rugged and isolated plateau, I could see the road stretching out for miles across the desert.
>
> In 1919, his family left Russia and moved to this country.
>
> In addition, staff members respond to queries, take new orders, and initiate billing.

7. If a sentence begins with an adverbial clause or phrase and can be easily read without a comma following it, writers will often omit the comma. In most cases where the comma is omitted, the phrase will be short—four words or less. But some writers will omit the comma even after a longer phrase if the sentence can be easily read or seems more forceful that way.

> In January the company will introduce a new line of entirely redesigned products.
>
> On the map the town appeared as a small dot in the midst of vast emptiness.
>
> If the project cannot be done profitably perhaps it should not be done at all.

8. Adverbial clauses and phrases that introduce a main clause other than the first main clause are usually set off with commas. However, if the adverbial clause or phrase follows a conjunction, style varies regarding how many commas are required to set it off. In most cases, two commas are used: one before the conjunction and one following the clause or phrase. Writers who prefer close punctuation usually use three commas: one before the conjunction and two more to enclose the clause or phrase. If the writer prefers open punctuation, the phrase may not be set off at all. In this case, only one comma that separates the main clauses is used. For more on open and close punctuation, see pages 3–4.

> His parents were against the match, and had the couple not eloped, their plans for marriage would have come to nothing.
>
> They have redecorated the entire store, but, to the delight of their customers, the store retains much of its original flavor. [close]

We haven't left Springfield yet, but when we get to Boston we'll call you. [open]

9. A comma is not used after an introductory phrase if the phrase immediately precedes the main verb.

In the road lay a dead rabbit.

10. Subordinate clauses and phrases that follow a main clause or that fall within a main clause are usually not set off by commas if they are restrictive. A clause or phrase is considered restrictive if its removal from the sentence would alter the meaning of the main clause. If the meaning of the main clause would not be altered by removing the subordinate clause or phrase, the clause or phrase is considered nonrestrictive and usually is set off by commas.

We will be delighted if she decides to stay. [restrictive]

Anyone who wants his or her copy of the book autographed by the author should get in line. [restrictive]

Her new book, *Fortune's Passage,* was well received. [nonrestrictive]

That was a good meal, although I didn't particularly like the broccoli in cream sauce. [nonrestrictive]

11. Commas are used to set off an adverbial clause or phrase that falls between the subject and the verb.

The weather, fluctuating from very hot to downright chilly, necessitated a variety of clothing.

12. Commas enclose modifying phrases that do not immediately precede the word or phrase they modify.

Hungry and tired, the soldiers marched back to camp.

We could see the importance, both long-term and short-term, of her proposal.

The two children, equally happy with their lunches, set off for school.

13. Absolute phrases are set off with commas, whether they fall at the beginning, middle, or end of the sentence.

Our business being concluded, we adjourned for refreshments.

We headed southward, the wind freshening behind us, to meet the rest of the fleet in the morning.

I still remember my first car, its bumpers sagging, its tires worn, its body rusting.

With Appositives

14. Commas are used to set off a word, phrase, or clause that is in apposition to a noun and that is nonrestrictive.

My husband, Larry, is in charge of ticket sales for the fair.

The highboy, or tallboy, is a tall chest of drawers typically made between 1690 and 1780.

George Washington, first president of the United States, has been the subject of countless biographies.

We were most impressed by the third candidate, the one who brought a writing sample and asked so many questions.

NOTE: A nonrestrictive appositive sometimes precedes the word with which it is in apposition. It is set off by commas in this position also.

A cherished landmark in the city, the Hotel Sandburg has managed once again to escape the wrecking ball.

15. Restrictive appositives are not set off by commas.

My daughter Andrea had the lead in the school play.

Alfred Hitchcock's thriller "Psycho" will be screened tonight.

With Introductory and Interrupting Elements

16. Commas set off transitional words and phrases (as *finally, meanwhile,* and *after all*).

Indeed, close coordination between departments can minimize confusion during this period of expansion.

We are eager to begin construction; however, the necessary materials have not yet arrived.

The most recent report, on the other hand, makes clear why the management avoids such agreements.

NOTE: Adverbs that can serve as transitional words can often serve in other ways as well. When these adverbs are not used to make a transition, no comma is necessary.

The materials had finally arrived.

17. Commas set off parenthetical elements, such as authorial asides and supplementary information, that are closely related to the rest of the sentence.

All of us, to tell the truth, were completely amazed by his suggestion.

The headmaster, now in his sixth year at the school, was responsible for the changes in the curriculum.

NOTE: When the parenthetical element is digressive or otherwise not closely related to the rest of the sentence, it is often set off by dashes or parentheses. For contrasting examples, see paragraph 3 under Dash and paragraphs 1 and 9 under Parentheses in this chapter.

18. Commas are used to set off words or phrases that introduce examples or explanations.

> He expects to visit three countries this summer, namely, France, Spain, and Germany.
>
> I would like to develop a good, workable plan, i.e., one that would outline our goals and set a timetable for their accomplishment.

NOTE: Words and phrases such as *i.e., e.g., namely, for example,* and *that is* are often preceded by a dash, open parenthesis, or semicolon, depending on the magnitude of the break in continuity represented by the examples or explanations that they introduce; however, regardless of the punctuation that precedes the word or phrase, a comma always follows it. For contrasting examples of dashes, parentheses, and semicolons with these words and phrases, see paragraph 6 under Dash, paragraph 2 under Parentheses, and paragraph 6 under Semicolon in this chapter.

19. Commas are used to set off words in direct address.

> We would like to discuss your account, Mrs. Reid.
>
> The answer, my friends, lies within us.

20. Commas set off mild interjections or exclamations such as *ah* or *oh*.

> Ah, summer—season of sunshine and goodwill.
> Oh, what a beautiful baby.

NOTE: The vocative *O* is not set off by commas.

> O Time! O Death!
> Have mercy, O Lord.

With Contrasting Expressions

21. A comma is used to set off contrasting expressions within a sentence.

> This project will take six months, not six weeks.
> He has merely changed his style, not his ethics.

22. Style varies regarding use of the comma to set off contrasting phrases used to describe a single word that follows immediately. In open punctuation, a comma follows the first modifier but is not used between the final modifier and the word modified. In close punctuation, the contrasting phrase is treated as a nonrestrictive modifier and is both preceded and followed by a comma. For more on open and close punctuation, see pages 3–4.

> The harsh, although eminently realistic critique is not going to make you popular. [open]
> The harsh, although eminently realistic, critique is not going to make you popular. [close]
> This street takes you away from, not toward the capitol building. [open]
> This street takes you away from, not toward, the capitol building. [close]

23. Adjectives and adverbs that modify the same word or phrase and that are joined by *but* or some other coordinating conjunction are not separated by a comma.

> a bicycle with a light but sturdy frame
> a multicolored but subdued rag rug
> errors caused by working carelessly or too quickly

24. A comma does not usually separate elements that are contrasted through the use of a pair of correlative conjunctions (as *either . . . or, neither . . . nor,* and *not only . . . but also*).

> The cost is either $69.95 or $79.95.
>
> Neither my brother nor I noticed the mistake.
>
> He was given the post not only because of his diplomatic connections but also because of his great tact and charm.

NOTE: Correlative conjunctions are sometimes used to join main clauses. If the clauses are short, a comma is not added; however, if the clauses are long, a comma usually separates them.

> Either you do it my way or we don't do it at all.
>
> Not only did she have to see three salesmen and a visiting reporter during the course of the day, but she also had to prepare for the next day's meeting with the president.

25. Long parallel contrasting and comparing clauses are separated by commas; short parallel phrases are not.

The more I heard about this new project, the greater was my desire to volunteer.

"The sooner the better," I said.

With Items in a Series

26. Words, phrases, and clauses joined in a series are separated by commas. If main clauses are joined in a series, they may be separated by either semicolons or commas. For more on the use of commas and semicolons to separate main clauses, see paragraphs 1, 3, and 4 above and paragraph 5 under Semicolon in this chapter.

> Men, women, and children crowded aboard the train.
>
> Her job required her to pack quickly, to travel often, and to have no personal life.
>
> He responded patiently while reporters shouted questions, flashbulbs popped, and the crowd pushed closer.

NOTE: Style varies regarding the use of the comma between the last two items in a series if those items are also joined by a conjunction. In some cases, as in the example below, omitting the final comma (often called the serial comma) can result in ambiguity. Some writers feel that in most sentences the use of the conjunction makes the comma superfluous, and they favor using the comma only when a misreading could result from omitting it. Others feel that it is easier to include the final comma routinely rather than try to consider each sentence separately to decide whether a misreading is possible without the comma. Most reference books, including this one, and most other book-length works of nonfiction use the serial comma. In all other categories of publishing, according to our evidence, usage is evenly or nearly evenly divided on the use or omission of this comma.

> We are looking for a house with a big yard, a view of the harbor, and beach and docking privileges. [with serial comma]
>
> We are looking for a house with a big yard, a view of the harbor and beach and docking privileges. [without serial comma]

27. A comma is not used to separate items in a series that are joined with conjunctions.

> I don't understand what this policy covers or doesn't cover or only partially covers.
>
> I have talked to the president and the vice president and three other executives.

28. When the elements in a series are long or complex or consist of clauses that themselves contain commas, the elements are usually separated by semicolons, not commas. For more on this use of the semicolon, see paragraphs 7 and 8 under Semicolon in this chapter.

With Compound Modifiers

29. A comma is used to separate two or more adjectives, adverbs, or phrases that modify the same word or phrase. For the use of commas with contrasting modifiers, see paragraphs 22 and 23 above.

She spoke in a calm, reflective manner.

We watched the skier move smoothly, gracefully through the turns.

His story was too fantastic, too undersupported by facts for us to take seriously.

30. A comma is not used between two adjectives when the first modifies the combination of the second adjective plus the word or phrase it modifies.

> a little brown jug
> a modern concrete-and-glass building

31. A comma is not used to separate an adverb from the adjective or adverb that it modifies.

> a truly distinctive manner
> running very quickly down the street

In Quotations, Questions, and Indirect Discourse

32. A comma separates a direct quotation from a phrase identifying its source or speaker. If the quotation is a question or an exclamation and the identifying phrase follows the quotation, the comma is replaced by a question mark or an exclamation point.

> Mary said, "I am leaving."
> "I am leaving," Mary said.
> Mary asked, "Where are you going?"
> "Where are you going?" Mary asked.
> "I am leaving," Mary said, "even if you want me to stay."
> "Don't do that!" Mary shouted.

NOTE: In some cases, a colon can replace a comma preceding a quotation. For more on this use of the colon, see paragraph 6 under Colon in this chapter.

33. A comma does not set off a quotation that is tightly incorporated into the sentence in which it appears.

> Throughout the session his only responses were "No comment" and "I don't think so."
>
> Just because he said he was "about to leave this minute" doesn't mean he actually left.

34. Style varies regarding the use of commas to set off shorter sentences that fall within longer sentences and that do not constitute actual dialogue. These shorter sentences may be mottoes or maxims, unspoken or imaginary dialogue, or sentences referred to as sentences; and they may or may not be enclosed in quotation marks. (For more on the use of quotation marks with sentences like these, see paragraph 6 under Quotation Marks, Double, in this chapter.) Typically the shorter sentence functions as a subject, object, or complement within the larger sentence and does not require a comma. Sometimes the structure of the larger sentence will be styled like actual quoted dialogue, and in such cases a comma is used to separate the shorter sentence from the text that introduces or identifies it. In some cases, where an author decides not to use quotation marks, a comma may be inserted simply to mark the beginning of the shorter sentence clearly.

"The computer is down" was the response she dreaded.

Another confusing idiom is "How do you do?"

He spoke with a candor that seemed to insist, This actually happened to me and in just this way.

The first rule is, When in doubt, spell it out.

When the shorter sentence functions as an appositive in the larger sentence, it is set off with a comma when nonrestrictive and not when restrictive. (For more on restrictive modifiers and appositives, see paragraphs 10, 14, and 15 above.)

He was fond of the slogan "Every man a king, but no man wears a crown."

We had the club's motto, "We make waves," printed on our T-shirts.

35. A comma introduces a direct question regardless of whether it is enclosed in quotation marks or if its first word is capitalized.

I wondered, what is going on here?

The question is, How do we get out of here?

What bothered her was, who had eaten all of the cookies?

36. The comma is omitted before quotations that are very short exclamations or representations of sounds.

He jumped up suddenly and cried "Yow!"

When she was done, she let out a loud "Whew!"

37. A comma is not used to set off indirect discourse or indirect questions introduced by a conjunction (such as *that* or *what*).

> Mary said that she was leaving.
>
> I wondered what was going on there.
>
> The clerk told me that the book I had ordered had just come in.

With Omitted Words

38. A comma indicates the omission of a word or phrase, especially in parallel constructions where the omitted word or phrase appears earlier in the sentence.

> Common stocks are preferred by some investors; bonds, by others.

39. A comma often replaces the conjunction *that*.

> The road was so steep and winding, we thought for sure that we would go over the edge.
>
> The problem is, we don't know how to fix it.

With Addresses, Dates, and Numbers

40. A comma is used to set off the individual elements of an address except for zip codes. In current practice, no punctuation appears between a state name and the zip code that follows it. If prepositions are used between the elements of the address, commas are not needed.

> Mrs. Bryant may be reached at 52 Kiowa Circle, Mesa, Arizona.

Mr. Briscoe was born in Liverpool, England.

The collection will be displayed at the Wilmington, Delaware, Museum of Art.

Write to the Bureau of the Census, Washington, DC 20233.

The White House is located at 1600 Pennsylvania Avenue in Washington, D.C.

NOTE: Some writers omit the comma that follows the name of a state when no other element of an address follows it. This is most likely to happen when a city name and state name are being used in combination to modify a noun that follows; however, our evidence indicates that retaining this comma is still the more common practice.

We visited their Enid, Oklahoma plant.
   but more commonly
We visited their Enid, Oklahoma, plant.

41. Commas are used to set off the year from the day of the month. When only the month and the year are given, the comma is usually omitted.

On October 26, 1947, the newly hired employees began work on the project.

In December 1903, the Wright brothers finally succeeded in keeping an airplane aloft for a few seconds.

42. A comma groups numerals into units of three to separate thousands, millions, and so on; however, this comma is generally not used in page numbers, street numbers, or numbers within dates. For more on the styling of numbers, see Chapter 5, "The Treatment of Numbers."

a population of 350,000
the year 1986
4509 South Pleasant Street
page 1419

With Names, Degrees, and Titles

43. A comma punctuates an inverted name.

Sagan, Deborah J.

44. A comma is used between a surname and *Junior,*
Senior, or their abbreviations.

Morton A. Williams, Jr.
Douglas Fairbanks, Senior

45. A comma is often used to set off the word *Incorpo-*
rated or the abbreviation *Inc.* from the rest of a corporate name; however, many companies elect to
omit this comma from their names.

Leedy Manufacturing Company, Incorporated
Tektronics, Inc.
Merz-Fortunata Inc.

46. A comma separates a surname from a following academic, honorary, military, or religious degree or
title.

Amelia P. Artandi, D.V.M.
John L. Farber, Esq.
Sister Mary Catherine, S.C.
Robert Menard, MpA., Ph.D.
Admiral Herman Washington, USN

In Correspondence

47. The comma follows the salutation in informal correspondence and follows the complimentary close in both informal and formal correspondence. In formal correspondence, a colon follows the salutation. For more on this use of the colon, see paragraph 12 under Colon in this chapter.

> Dear Rachel,
> Affectionately,
> Very truly yours,

Other Uses

48. The comma is used to avoid ambiguity when the juxtaposition of two words or expressions could cause confusion.

> Whatever will be, will be.
> To John, Marshall was someone special.
> I repaired the lamp that my brother had broken, and replaced the bulb.

49. A comma often follows a direct object or a predicate nominative or predicate adjective when they precede the subject and verb in the sentence. If the meaning of the sentence is clear without this comma, it is often omitted.

> That we would soon have to raise prices, no one disputed.
> Critical about the current state of affairs, we might have been.
> A disaster it certainly was.

With Other Marks of Punctuation

50. Commas are used in conjunction with brackets, ellipsis points, parentheses, and quotation marks. Commas are not used in conjunction with colons, dashes, exclamation points, question marks, or semicolons. If one of these latter marks falls at the same point in a sentence at which a comma would fall, the comma is dropped and the other mark is retained. For more on the use of commas with other marks of punctuation, see the heading With Other Marks of Punctuation in the sections of this chapter covering those marks of punctuation.

Dash

In many of its uses, the dash functions like a comma, a colon, or a pair of parentheses. Like commas and parentheses, dashes set off parenthetic material such as examples, supplemental facts, or appositional, explanatory, or descriptive phrases. Like colons, dashes introduce clauses that explain or expand upon some element of the material that precedes them. The dash is sometimes considered to be a less formal equivalent of the colon and parenthesis, and it does frequently take their place in advertising and other informal contexts. However, dashes are prevalent in all kinds of writing, including the most formal, and the choice of which mark to use is usually a matter of personal preference.

The dash exists in a number of different lengths. The dash in most general use is the em dash, which is approximately the width of an uppercase M in typeset material. In typewritten material, it is represented by two hyphens. The en dash and the two- and three-em dashes have more limited uses which are explained in paragraphs 15–18 below.

Abrupt Change or Suspension

1. The dash marks an abrupt change in the flow of a writer's thought or in the structure of a sentence.

   > The mountain that we climbed is higher than—well, never mind how high it is.
   > The students seemed happy with the change, but the alumni—there was the problem.

2. Dashes mark a suspension in the writer's flow of thought or in the sentence structure. Such suspensions are frequently caused by an authorial aside.

   > He was—how shall we put it?—a controversial character to say the least.
   > If I had kept my notes—and I really wish that I had—I would be able to give you the exact date of the sale.

Parenthetic and Amplifying Elements

3. Dashes are used in place of other punctuation (such as commas or parentheses) to emphasize parenthetic or amplifying material or to make such material stand out more clearly from the rest of the sentence.

She is willing to discuss all problems—those she has solved and those for which there is no immediate solution.

In 1976, they asked for—and received—substantial grants from the federal government.

The privately owned consulting firm—formerly known as Aborjaily and Associates—is now offering many new services.

NOTE: When dashes are used to set off parenthetic elements, they often indicate that the material is more digressive than elements set off with commas but less digressive than elements set off by parentheses. For contrasting examples see paragraph 17 under Comma and paragraphs 1 and 9 under Parentheses in this chapter.

4. Dashes are used to set off or to introduce defining and enumerating phrases.

The fund sought to acquire controlling positions—a minimum of 25% of outstanding voting securities—in other companies.

The essay dealt with our problems with waste—cans, bottles, discarded tires, and other trash.

5. A dash is often used in place of a colon or semicolon to link clauses, especially when the clause that follows the dash explains, summarizes, or expands upon the clause that precedes it.

The test results were surprisingly good—none of the tested models displayed serious problems.

The deterioration of our bridges and roads has been apparent for many years—parts of the interstate high-

way system are 30 years old, after all, and most of our
bridges are older than that.

6. A dash or a pair of dashes often sets off parenthetic or amplifying material introduced by such
phrases as *for example, namely, that is, e.g.,* and *i.e.*

After some discussion the motion was tabled—that is,
it was removed indefinitely from the board's consider-
ation.

Sports develop two valuable traits—namely, self-
control and the ability to make quick decisions.

Not all "prime" windows—i.e., the ones installed when
a house is built—are equal in quality.

NOTE: Commas, parentheses, and semicolons are
often used for the same purpose. For contrasting
examples, see paragraph 18 under Comma, paragraph 2 under Parentheses, and paragraph 6 under Semicolon in this chapter.

7. A dash introduces a summary statement that follows a series of words or phrases.

Unemployment, strikes, inflation, stock prices, mort-
gage rates—all are part of the economy.

Once into bankruptcy, the company would have to
pay cash for its supplies, defer maintenance, and lay
off workers—moves that could threaten its long-term
profitability.

As a Mechanical Device

8. A dash precedes the name of an author or source
at the end of a quoted passage.

> Winter tames man, woman and beast.
>
> —William Shakespeare

> "A comprehensive, authoritative, and beautifully written biography."—*National Review*

NOTE: This method of attribution is most often used when the quoted material is not part of the main text. Examples of such situations are quotations set as epigraphs and quotations set as extracts. The attribution may appear immediately after the quotation, or it may appear on the next line.

9. A dash is used to indicate interrupted speech or a speaker's confusion or hesitation.

> "The next point I'd like to bring up—" the speaker started to say. "I'm sorry. I'll have to stop you there," the moderator broke in.
>
> "Yes," he went on, "yes—that is—I guess I agree."

NOTE: There is some disagreement among style manuals regarding the use of a comma between a quotation ending with a dash and its attribution. Our evidence indicates that the comma is usually omitted in such circumstances. This follows the general practice regarding the use of commas with dashes described in paragraph 11 below.

10. Dashes are used variously as elements in page design. They may, for example, precede items in a vertical enumeration, set off elements in the dateline of a newspaper report, or separate words from their definitions in a glossary. The use of dashes in such circumstances is usually determined by the editor or designer of the publication.

Required skills are:
—Shorthand
—Typing
—Transcription

With Other Marks of Punctuation

11. If a dash appears at a point in a sentence where a comma could also appear, the dash is retained and the comma is dropped. For one situation in which this practice is not always followed, see paragraph 9 above.

    If we don't succeed—and the critics say we won't—then the whole project is in jeopardy.

    Our lawyer has read the transcript—all 1200 pages of it—and he has decided that an appeal would not be useful.

    Some of the other departments, however—particularly Accounting, Sales, and Credit Collection—have expanded their computer operations.

12. If the second of a pair of dashes appears at a point in a sentence where a period or semicolon would also appear, the period or semicolon is retained and the dash is dropped.

    His conduct has always been exemplary—near-perfect attendance, excellent productivity, a good attitude; nevertheless, his termination cannot be avoided.

13. Dashes are used with exclamation points and question marks. When a pair of dashes sets off parenthetic material calling for either of these marks of

punctuation, the exclamation point or the question mark is placed inside the second dash. If the parenthetic material falls at the end of a sentence ending with an exclamation point or question mark, the closing dash is not required.

> His hobby was getting on people's nerves—especially mine!—and he was extremely good at it.
>
> When the committee meets next week—are you going to be there?—I will present all of the final figures.
>
> Is there any way to predict the future course of this case—one which we really cannot afford to lose?

14. Dashes and parentheses are used in combination to indicate parenthetic material appearing within parenthetic material. Our evidence indicates that dashes within parentheses and parentheses within dashes occur with about equal frequency.

> We were looking for a narrator (or narrators—sometimes a script calls for more than one) who could handle a variety of assignments.
>
> On our trip south we crossed a number of major rivers—the Hudson, the Delaware, and the Patapsco (which flows through Baltimore)—without paying a single toll.

NOTE: If the inner parenthetic element begins with a dash and its closing dash would fall in the same position as the closing parenthesis, the closing dash is omitted and the parenthesis is retained, as in the first example above. If the inner phrase begins with a parenthesis and its closing parenthesis would coincide with the closing dash, the closing parenthesis and the closing dash are both retained, as in the second example above.

En Dash

15. En dashes appear only in typeset material. The en dash is shorter than the em dash but slightly longer than the hyphen, and it is used in place of the hyphen in some situations. The most common use of the en dash is as an equivalent to "(up) to and including" when used between numbers, dates, or other notations that indicate range.

> 1984–85
> 8:30 a.m.–4:30 p.m.
> GS 12–14
> $20–$40
> Monday–Friday
> ages 10–15
> levels D–G
> 35–40 years
> pages 128–34

NOTE: The use of the en dash to replace the hyphen in such cases, although urged by most style manuals, is by no means universal. Writers and editors who wish to have en dashes set in their copy need to indicate on their manuscripts which hyphens should be set as en dashes, and this need to mark en dashes can obviously be an inconvenience and an invitation to errors. However, many writers and editors prefer to use en dashes because of the visual clarity they provide between numbers and because of the distinction they make between en dashes used to mean "to" and hyphens used to connect elements in compound words.

16. Publishers make various uses of the en dash, and no one set of rules can be said to be standard.

Some common uses of the en dash include using it as a replacement for the hyphen following a prefix that is added to an open compound, as a replacement for the word *to* between capitalized names, and to indicate linkages, such as boundaries, treaties, or oppositions.

> pre–Civil War architecture
> the New York–Connecticut area
> Chicago–Memphis train
> Washington–Moscow diplomacy
> the Dempsey–Tunney fight

Long Dashes

17. A two-em dash is used to indicate missing letters in a word and, less frequently, to indicate a missing word.

> Mr. P—— of Baltimore
> That's b——t and you know it.

18. A three-em dash indicates that a word has been left out or that an unknown word or figure is to be supplied. For the use of this dash in bibliography listings, see Chapter 6, "Notes and Bibliographies," pages 251–296.

> The study was carried out in _____, a fast-growing Sunbelt city.
> We'll leave New York City on the _____ of August.

Spacing

19. Style varies as to spacing around the dash. Some publications insert a space before and after the dash, others do not. Our evidence indicates that

the majority of publishers style the dash without spaces.

Ellipsis Points

Ellipsis points is the name most often given to periods when they are used, usually in groups of three, to signal an omission from quoted material or to indicate a pause or trailing off of speech. Other names for periods used in this way include *ellipses, points of ellipsis,* and *suspension points.* Ellipsis points are often used in conjunction with other marks of punctuation, including periods used to mark the ends of sentences. When ellipsis points are used in this way with a terminal period, the omission is sometimes thought of as being marked by four periods. Most of the conventions described in this section are illustrated with quoted material enclosed in quotation marks. However, the conventions are equally applicable to quoted material set as extracts.

> NOTE: The examples given below present passages in which ellipsis points indicate omission of material. In most cases, the full text from which these omissions have been made is some portion of the headnote above.

1. Ellipsis points indicate the omission of one or more words within a quoted sentence.

   > One book said, "Other names ... include *ellipses, points of ellipsis,* and *suspension points.*"

2. Ellipsis points are usually not used to indicate the omission of words that precede the quoted portion. However, style varies on this point, and in some formal contexts, especially those in which the quotation is introduced by a colon, ellipsis points are used.

> The book maintained that "the omission is sometimes thought of as being marked by four periods."
>
> The book maintained: ". . . the omission is sometimes thought of as being marked by four periods."

3. Punctuation used in the original that falls on either side of the ellipsis points is often omitted; however, it may be retained, especially if such retention helps clarify the sentence.

> According to the book, "*Ellipsis points* is the name most often given to periods when they are used . . . to signal an omission from quoted material or to indicate a pause or trailing off of speech."
>
> According to the book, "When ellipsis points are used in this way . . . , the omission is sometimes thought of as being marked by four periods."
>
> According to the book, "*Ellipsis points* is the name most often given to periods when they are used, usually in groups of three; . . . to indicate a pause or trailing off of speech."

4. If an omission comprises an entire sentence within a passage, the last part of a sentence within a passage, or the first part of a sentence other than the first quoted sentence, the end punctuation preceding or following the omission is retained and is followed by three periods.

That book says, "Other names for periods used in this way include *ellipses, points of ellipsis,* and *suspension points.* . . . When ellipsis points are used in this way with a terminal period, the omission is sometimes thought of as being marked by four periods."

That book says, "*Ellipsis points* is the name given to periods when they are used, usually in groups of three, to signal an omission from quoted material. . . . Other names for periods used in this way include *ellipses, points of ellipsis,* and *suspension points.*"

That book says, "Ellipsis points are often used in conjunction with other marks of punctuation, including periods used to mark ends of sentences. . . . The omission is sometimes thought of as being marked by four periods."

NOTE: The capitalization of the word *The* in the third example is acceptable. When the opening words of a quotation act as a sentence within the quotation, the first word is capitalized, even if that word did not begin a sentence in the original version.

5. If the last words of a quoted sentence are omitted and if the original sentence ends with a period, that period is retained and three ellipsis points follow. However, if the original sentence ends with punctuation other than a period, the end punctuation often follows the ellipsis points, especially if it helps clarify the quotation.

Their book said, "Ellipsis points are often used in conjunction with other marks of punctuation. . . ."

He always ends his harangues with some variation on the question, "What could you have been thinking when you . . . ?"

NOTE: Many writers and editors, especially those writing in more informal contexts, choose to ignore the styling considerations presented in paragraphs 4 and 5. They use instead an alternative system in which all omissions are indicated by three periods and all terminal periods that may precede or follow an omission are dropped.

6. Ellipsis points are used to indicate that a quoted sentence has been intentionally left unfinished. In situations such as this the terminal period is not included.

> Read the statement beginning *"Ellipsis points* is the name most often given . . ." and then proceed to the numbered paragraphs.

7. When a full line or several consecutive lines of poetry are omitted from a quotation, the omission is indicated by a line of spaced points. The lines of points extend the length of the preceding line or of the missing line.

> Whitman's attitude on the subject is revealed in these lines from "When I Heard the Learned Astronomer":
> When I heard the learned astronomer,
> . . . .
> How soon unaccountable I became tired and sick,
> Til rising and gliding out I wandered off by myself,
> In the mystical moist night-air, and from time to time,
> Looked up in perfect silence at the stars.

NOTE: Style varies regarding the treatment of poetry quotations that do not end in a period. Sometimes authors indicate an omission with ellipsis points, sometimes they prefer not to use ellipsis points but rather to reproduce the text exactly as it appeared in the original version.

> Whitman's attitude on the subject is revealed in these lines from "When I Heard the Learned Astronomer":
>
> When I heard the learned astronomer,
> ....
> How soon unaccountable I became tired and sick, ...
>
> Whitman's attitude on the subject is revealed in these lines from "When I Heard the Learned Astronomer":
>
> When I heard the learned astronomer,
> ....
> How soon unaccountable I became tired and sick,

8. Ellipsis points are used to indicate faltering speech, especially if the faltering involves a long pause between words or a sentence that trails off or is left intentionally unfinished. In these kinds of sentences most writers treat the ellipsis points as terminal punctuation, thus removing the need for any other punctuation; however, style does vary on this point, and some writers routinely use other punctuation in conjunction with ellipsis points.

> The speaker seemed uncertain how to answer the question. "Well, that's true ... but even so ... I think we can do better."
>
> "Despite these uncertainties, we believe we can do it, but ..."
>
> "I mean ..." he said, "like ... How?"

9. Ellipsis points are sometimes used as a stylistic device to catch and hold a reader's attention.

> They think that nothing can go wrong ... but it does.

10. Each ellipsis point is set off from other ellipsis points, from adjacent punctuation (except for quotation marks, which are closed up to the ellipsis points), and from surrounding text by a space. If a terminal period is used with ellipsis points, it precedes them with no space before it and one space after it.

Exclamation Point

The exclamation point is used to mark a forceful comment. Writers and editors usually try to avoid using the exclamation point too frequently, because its heavy use can weaken its effect.

1. An exclamation point can punctuate a sentence, phrase, or interjection.

> This is the fourth time in a row he's missed his cue!
>
> No one that I talked to—not even the accounting department!—seemed to know how the figures were calculated.
>
> Oh! you startled me.
>
> Ah, those eyes!

2. The exclamation point replaces the question mark when an ironic or emphatic tone is more important than the actual question.

Aren't you finished yet!
Do you realize what you've done!
Why me!

3. Occasionally the exclamation point is used with a question mark to indicate a very forceful question.

How much did you say?!
You did what!?

NOTE: The interrobang, printed ‽ , was created to punctuate the types of sentences described in paragraphs 2 and 3 above. However, the character is not available to most typesetters, and it is rarely used.

4. In mathematical expressions, the exclamation point indicates a factorial.

$$n! \cdot m! \geq (n)(m!)$$

5. The exclamation point is enclosed within brackets, dashes, parentheses, and quotation marks when it punctuates the material so enclosed rather than the sentence as a whole. It should be placed outside them when it punctuates the entire sentence.

All of this proves—at long last!—that we were right from the start.
Somehow the dog got the gate open (for the third time!) and ran into the street.
He shouted, "Wait!" and sprinted toward the train.
The correct word is "mousse," not "moose"!

6. Exclamatory phrases that occur within a sentence are set off by dashes or parentheses.

> And now our competition—get this!—wants to start sharing secrets.
>
> The board accepted most of the recommendations, but ours (alas!) was not even considered.

7. If an exclamation point falls at a place in a sentence where a comma or a terminal period could also go, the comma or period is dropped and the exclamation point is retained.

> "Absolutely not!" he snapped.
>
> She has written about sixty pages so far—and with no help!

NOTE: If the exclamation point is part of a title, as of a play, book, or movie, it may be followed by a comma. If the title falls at the end of a sentence, the terminal period is usually dropped.

> Marshall and Susan went to see the musical *Oklahoma!*, and they enjoyed it very much.
>
> They enjoyed seeing the musical *Oklahoma!*

8. In typewritten material, two spaces follow an exclamation point that ends a sentence. If the exclamation point is followed by a closing bracket, closing parenthesis, or closing quotation marks, the two spaces follow the second mark. In typeset material, only one space follows the exclamation point.

```
The time is now!  Decide what you are
going to do.
She said, "The time is now!"  That meant
we had to decide what to do.
```

The time is now! Decide what you are going to do.
She said, "The time is now!" That meant we had to
decide what to do.

Hyphen

1. Hyphens are used to link elements in compound
   words. For more on the styling of compound
   words, see the section on Compounds, beginning
   on page 157, in Chapter 3, "Plurals, Possessives,
   and Compounds."

2. A hyphen marks an end-of-line division of a word
   when part of the word is to be carried down to the
   next line.

   > Unemployment, strikes, inflation, stock prices, mort-
   > gage rates—all are part of the economy.

3. A hyphen divides letters or syllables to give the effect of stuttering, sobbing, or halting speech.

   > S-s-sammy
   > ah-ah-ah
   > y-y-es

4. Hyphens indicate a word spelled out letter by
   letter.

   > p-r-o-b-a-t-i-o-n

5. A hyphen indicates that a word element is a prefix, suffix, or medial element.

   anti-
   -ship
   -o-

6. A hyphen is used in typewritten material as an equivalent to the phrase "(up) to and including" when placed between numbers and dates. In typeset material this hyphen is very often replaced by an en dash. For more on the use of the en dash, see paragraphs 15 and 16 under Dash in this chapter.

7. Hyphens are sometimes used to produce inflected forms of verbs that are made of individually pronounced letters or to add an *-er* ending to an abbreviation; however, apostrophes are more commonly used for this purpose. For more on these uses of the apostrophe, see paragraphs 6 and 7 under Apostrophe in this chapter.

   D.H.-ing for the White Sox
   a loyal AA-er

Parentheses

Parentheses enclose supplementary elements that are inserted into a main statement but that are not intended to be part of the statement; in fact, parenthetic elements often interrupt the main structure of the sentence. For some of the cases described below, especially those listed under the heading "Parenthetic Elements," commas and dashes are frequently used instead of parentheses. (For contrasting examples, see paragraph 17 under Comma and paragraph 3 under Dash in this chapter.) In general, commas tend to be used when the inserted material is closely related, logically or grammatically, to the main clause; parentheses are more often used when the inserted material is incidental or digressive. Some newspapers and news magazines avoid the use of parentheses in straight news reporting and rely instead on the dash. In most cases, however, the choice of dashes or parentheses to enclose parenthetic material is a matter of personal preference.

Parenthetic Elements

1. Parentheses enclose phrases and clauses that provide examples, explanations, or supplementary facts. Supplementary numerical data may also be enclosed in parentheses.

> Nominations for the association's principal officers (president, vice president, treasurer, and secretary) were heard and approved at the last meeting.

> Although we liked the restaurant (their Italian food was the best), we seldom went there.

> Three old destroyers (all now out of commission) will be scrapped.

> Their first baseman was hitting well that season (.297, 84 RBIs), and their left fielder was doing well also (21 HRs, 78 RBIs).

2. Parentheses enclose phrases and clauses introduced by expressions such as *namely, that is, e.g.,* and *i.e.* Commas, dashes, and semicolons are also used to perform this function. (For contrasting examples, see paragraph 18 under Comma, paragraph 6 under Dash, and paragraph 6 under Semicolon in this chapter.)

> In writing to the manufacturer, be as specific as possible (i.e., list the missing or defective parts, describe the nature of the malfunction, and provide the name and address of the store where the unit was purchased).

3. Parentheses set off definitions, translations, or alternate names for words in the main part of a sentence.

> The company sold off all of its retail outlets and announced plans to sell off its houseware (small appliance) business as well.

> He has followed the fortunes of the modern renaissance (*al-Nahdad*) in the Arab-speaking world.

> The hotel was located just a few blocks from San Antonio's famous Paseo del Rio (river walk).

> They were scheduled to play Beethoven's Trio in B-flat major, Opus 97 ("The Archduke").

4. Parentheses enclose abbreviations synonymous with spelled-out forms and occurring after those forms, or they may enclose the spelled-out form occurring after the abbreviation.

> She referred to a ruling by the Federal Communications Commission (FCC).

They were involved with a study regarding the manufacture and disposal of PVC (polyvinyl chloride).

5. Parentheses are used in running text to set off bibliographical or historical data about books, articles, or other published or artistic works. For full information regarding the use of parentheses with bibliographical references, see the section on Parenthetical References, beginning on page 269, in Chapter 6, "Notes and Bibliographies."

> His work was influenced by several of Freud's essays, including "Some Character Types Met with in Psychoanalytic Work" (1916).
>
> *Ohio Impromptu* (1981) was written for a special performance at Ohio State University.
>
> Another book in this category is Alice Schick's *Serengeti Cats* (Lippincott, $10.53).

6. Parentheses often set off cross-references.

> Telephone ordering service is also provided (refer to the list of stores at the end of this catalog).
>
> Textbooks are available at the bookstore for all on-campus courses. (See page 12 for hours.)
>
> The diagram (Fig. 3) illustrates the action of the pump.

7. Parentheses enclose Arabic numerals that confirm a spelled-out number in a text.

> Delivery will be made in thirty (30) days.

8. Parentheses enclose the name of a city or state that is inserted into a proper name for identification.

the Norristown (Pa.) State Hospital
the *Tulsa* (Okla.) *Tribune*

9. Some writers use parentheses to set off personal asides.

It was largely as a result of this conference that the committee was formed (its subsequent growth in influence is another story).

10. Parentheses are used to set off quotations, either attributed or unattributed, that illustrate or support a statement made in the main text.

After he had had a few brushes with the police, his stepfather had him sent to jail as an incorrigible ("It will do him good").

As a Mechanical Device

11. Parentheses enclose unpunctuated numbers or letters in a series within running text.

We must set forth (1) our long-term goals, (2) our immediate objectives, and (3) the means at our disposal.

NOTE: Some writers and editors use only a single parenthesis following the number; however, most style books advise that parentheses be used both before and after, and most publications do follow that style.

12. Parentheses indicate alternative terms.

Please indicate the lecture(s) you would like to attend.

13. Parentheses are used in combination with numbers for several mechanical purposes, such as setting off area codes in telephone numbers, indicating losses in accounting, and grouping elements in mathematical expressions.

(413) 256-7899
$3(a+b) + 4(a+b)$

Operating Profits (in millions)

Cosmetics	26.2
Food products	47.7
Food services	54.3
Transportation	(17.7)
Sporting goods	(11.2)
Total	99.3

With Other Marks of Punctuation

14. If a parenthetic expression is an independent sentence, its first word is capitalized and a period is placed *inside* the last parenthesis. On the other hand, a parenthetic expression that occurs within a sentence—even if it could stand alone as a separate sentence—does not end with a period. It may, however, end with an exclamation point, a question mark, a period after an abbreviation, or a set of quotation marks. A parenthetic expression within a sentence does not require capitalization unless it is a quoted sentence. (For more on the use of capitals with parenthetic expressions, see the section on Beginnings, starting on page 92, in Chapter 2, "Capitals, Italics, and Quotation Marks.")

The discussion was held in the boardroom. (The results are still confidential.)

Although several trade organizations worked actively against the legislation (there were at least three paid lobbyists working on Capitol Hill at any one time), the bill passed easily.

After waiting in line for an hour (why do we do these things?), we finally left.

The conference was held in Vancouver (that's in B.C.).

He was totally confused ("What can we do?") and refused to see anyone.

15. If a parenthetic expression within a sentence is composed of two independent clauses, capitalization and periods are avoided. To separate the clauses within the parentheses, semicolons are usually used. If the parenthetic expression occurs outside of a sentence, normal patterns of capitalization and punctuation prevail.

We visited several showrooms, looked at the prices (it wasn't a pleasant experience; prices in this area have not gone down), and asked all the questions we could think of.

We visited several showrooms and looked at the prices. (It wasn't a pleasant experience. Prices in this area have not gone down.) If salespeople were available, we asked all of the questions we could think of.

16. No punctuation mark (other than a period after an abbreviation) is placed before parenthetic material within a sentence; if a break is required, the punctuation is placed after the final parenthesis.

I'll get back to you tomorrow (Friday), when I have more details.

17. Parentheses sometimes appear within parentheses, although the usual practice is to replace the inner pair of parentheses with a pair of brackets. (For an example of brackets within parentheses, see paragraph 6 under Brackets in this chapter.)

> Checks must be drawn in U.S. dollars. (PLEASE NOTE: In accordance with U.S. Department of Treasury regulations, we cannot accept checks drawn on Canadian banks for amounts less than four U.S. dollars ($4.00). The same regulation applies to Canadian money orders.)

18. Dashes and parentheses are often used together to set off parenthetic material within a larger parenthetic element. For details and examples, see paragraph 14 under Dash in this chapter.

Spacing

19. In typewritten material, a parenthetic expression that is an independent sentence is followed by two spaces. In typeset material, the sentence is followed by one space. In typewritten or typeset material, a parenthetic expression that falls within a sentence is followed by one space.

```
We visited several showrooms and looked
at the prices. (It wasn't a pleasant
experience.  Prices in this area have
not gone down.)  We asked all the
questions we could think of.
```

We visited several showrooms and looked at the prices. (It wasn't a pleasant experience. Prices in this area have not gone down.) We asked all the questions we could think of.

NOTE: Paragraphs 14 and 15 above are followed by examples that illustrate the appearance in typeset material of parenthetic expressions that are independent sentences.

Period

This section describes uses of the period in running text. For rules regarding use of the period in bibliographies, see Chapter 6, "Notes and Bibliographies." For the use of three periods to indicate a pause or omission, see the section on Ellipsis Points in this chapter.

1. A period terminates a sentence or a sentence fragment that is neither interrogative nor exclamatory.

   Do your best.
   I did my best.
   Total chaos. Nothing works.

2. A period punctuates some abbreviations. For more on the punctuation of abbreviations, see the section on Punctuation, beginning on page 188, in Chapter 4, "Abbreviations."

   a.k.a.
   fig.
   N.W.

Assn.
in.
U.S.
Dr.
No.
Inc.
Jr.
e.g.
Co.
Ph.D.
ibid.
Corp.

3. A period is used with an individual's initials. If all of the person's initials are used instead of the name, however, the unspaced initials may be written without periods.

F. Scott Fitzgerald
Susan B. Anthony
F.D.R. *or* FDR
T. S. Eliot

4. A period follows Roman and Arabic numerals and also letters when they are used without parentheses in outlines and vertical enumerations.

I. Objectives
  A. Economy
    1. Low initial cost
    2. Low maintenance cost
  B. Ease of operation

Required skills are:
  1. Shorthand
  2. Typing
  3. Transcription

5. A period is placed within quotation marks even when it does not punctuate the quoted material.

> The charismatic leader was known to his followers as "the guiding light."
>
> "I said I wanted to fire him," Henry went on, "but she said, 'I don't think you have the contractual privilege to do that.' "

6. When brackets or parentheses enclose a sentence that is independent of surrounding sentences, the period is placed inside the closing parenthesis or bracket. However, when brackets or parentheses enclose a sentence that is part of a surrounding sentence, the period for the enclosed sentence is omitted.

> On Friday the government ordered a 24-hour curfew and told all journalists and photographers to leave the area. (Authorities later confiscated the film of those who did not comply.)
>
> I took a good look at her (she was standing quite close to me at the time).

7. In typewritten material, two spaces follow a period that ends a sentence. If the period is followed by a closing bracket, closing parenthesis, or quotation marks, the two spaces follow the second mark. In typeset material, only one space follows this period.

> ```
> Here is the car.    Do you want to get in?
> He said, "Here is the car."    I asked if
> I should get in.
> ```
>
> Here is the car. Do you want to get in?

8. One space follows a period that comes after an initial in a name. If a name is composed entirely of initials, no space is required; however, the usual styling for such names is to omit the periods.

> Mr. H. C. Matthews
> F.D.R. *or* FDR

9. No space follows an internal period within a punctuated abbreviation.

> f.o.b.
> i.e.
> Ph.D.
> A.D.
> p.m.

Question Mark

1. The question mark terminates a direct question.

> What went wrong?
> "When do they arrive?" she asked.

NOTE: The intent of the writer, not the word order of the sentence, determines whether or not the sentence is a question. Polite requests that are worded as questions, for instance, usually take periods, because they are not really questions. Similarly, sentences whose word order is that of a statement but whose force is interrogatory are punctuated with question marks.

Will you please sit down.

He did that?

2. The question mark terminates an interrogative element that is part of a sentence. An indirect question is not followed by a question mark.

The old arithmetic books were full of How-much-wall-paper-will-it-take-to-cover-a-room? questions.

How did she do it? was the question on everybody's mind.

She wondered, will it work?

She wondered whether it would work.

3. The question mark punctuates each element of an interrogative series that is neither numbered nor lettered. When an interrogative series is numbered or lettered, only one question mark is used, and it is placed at the end of the series.

Can you give us a reasonable forecast? back up your predictions? compare them with last year's earnings?

Can you (1) give us a reasonable forecast, (2) back up your predictions, (3) compare them with last year's earnings?

4. The question mark indicates a writer's or editor's uncertainty about a fact.

Geoffrey Chaucer, English poet (1340?–1400)

5. The question mark is placed inside a closing bracket, dash, parenthesis, or pair of quotation marks when it punctuates only the material enclosed by that mark and not the sentence as a whole. It is placed outside that mark when it punctuates the entire sentence.

> What did Andrew mean when he called the project "a fiasco from the start"?

> I had a vacation in 1975 (was it really that long ago?), but I haven't had time for one since.

> "She thought about it for a moment," Alice continued, "and finally she said, 'Can you guarantee this will work?'"

> He asked, "Do you realize the extent of the problem [the housing shortage]?"

6. In typewritten material, two spaces follow a question mark that ends a sentence. If the question mark is followed by a closing bracket, closing parenthesis, or quotation marks, the two spaces follow the second mark. In typeset material, only one space follows the question mark.

> She wondered, will it work?   He said he thought it would.

> She asked, "Will it work?"   He said he thought it would.

> She wondered, will it work? He said he thought it would.

7. One space follows a question mark that falls within a sentence.

> Are you coming today? tomorrow? the day after?

Quotation Marks, Double

This section describes the use of quotation marks to enclose quoted matter in running text. It also describes
the mechanical uses of quotation marks, such as to set
off translations of words or to enclose single letters
within sentences. For the use of quotation marks to enclose titles of poems, paintings, or other works, see the
section on Proper Nouns, Pronouns, and Adjectives,
beginning on page 96, in Chapter 2, "Capitals,
Italics, and Quotation Marks."

> NOTE: Lengthy passages of quoted material are
> usually indented as separate paragraphs without
> enclosing quotation marks. These paragraphs are
> commonly referred to as *extracts, excerpts,* or *block
> quotations.* Typically, block quotations are preceded
> by a full sentence ending with a colon, and they be-
> gin with a full sentence whose first word is capital-
> ized. For an example of a block quotation, see
> paragraph 5 under Colon in this chapter.

Basic Uses

1. Quotation marks enclose direct quotations but not
   indirect quotations.

   > She said, "I am leaving."
   > "I am leaving," she said, "and I'm not coming back."
   > "I am leaving," she said. "This has gone on long
   > enough."
   > She said that she was leaving.

2. Quotation marks enclose fragments of quoted matter when they are reproduced exactly as originally stated.

> The agreement makes it clear that he "will be paid only upon receipt of an acceptable manuscript."
>
> As late as 1754, documents refer to him as "yeoman" and "husbandman."

3. Quotation marks enclose words or phrases borrowed from others, words used in a special way, or words of marked informality when they are introduced into formal writing.

> That kind of corporation is referred to as "closed" or "privately held."
>
> Be sure to send a copy of your résumé, or as some folks would say, your "biodata summary."
>
> They were afraid the patient had "stroked out"—had had a cerebrovascular accident.

4. Quotation marks are sometimes used to enclose words referred to as words. Italic type is also frequently used for this purpose. For more on this use of italics, see the section on Other Uses of Italics, beginning on page 134, in Chapter 2, "Capitals, Italics, and Quotation Marks."

> He went through the manuscript and changed every "he" to "she."

5. Quotation marks enclose short exclamations or representations of sounds. Representations of sounds are also frequently set in italic type. For more on this use of italics, see the section on Other

Uses of Italics, beginning on page 134, in Chapter 2, "Capitals, Italics, and Quotation Marks."

"Ssshh!" she hissed.
They never say anything crude like "shaddap."

6. Quotation marks enclose short sentences that fall within longer sentences, especially when the shorter sentence is meant to suggest spoken dialogue. Kinds of sentences that may be treated in this way include mottoes and maxims, unspoken or imaginary dialogue, or sentences referred to as sentences.

Throughout the camp, the spirit was "We can do."
She never could get used to his "That's the way it goes" attitude.
In effect, the voters were saying "You blew it, and you don't get another chance."
Their attitude could only be described as "Kill the messenger."
Another example of a palindrome is "Madam, I'm Adam."

NOTE: Style varies regarding the punctuation of sentences such as these. In general, the force of the quotation marks is to set the shorter sentence off more distinctly from the surrounding sentence and to give the shorter sentence more of the feel of spoken dialogue; omitting the quotation marks diminishes the effect. (For a description of the use of commas in sentences like these, see paragraphs 33 and 34 under Comma in this chapter.)

The first rule is, When in doubt, spell it out.

They weren't happy with the impression she left: "Don't expect favors, because I don't have to give them."

7. Quotation marks are not used to enclose paraphrases.

Build a better mouse trap, Emerson says, and the world will beat a path to your door.

8. Direct questions are usually not enclosed in quotation marks unless they represent quoted dialogue.

The question is, What went wrong?

As we listened to him, we couldn't help wondering, Where's the plan?

She asked, "What went wrong?"

NOTE: As in the sentences presented in paragraph 6 above, style varies regarding the use of quotation marks with direct questions; and in many cases, writers will include the quotation marks.

As we listened to him, we couldn't help wondering, "Where's the plan?"

9. Quotation marks are used to enclose translations of foreign or borrowed terms.

The term *sesquipedalian* comes from the Latin word *sesquipedalis*, meaning "a foot and a half long."

While in Texas, he encountered the armadillo ("little armored one") and developed quite an interest in it.

10. Quotation marks are sometimes used to enclose single letters within a sentence.

> The letter "m" is wider than the letter "i."
>
> We started to work on the dictionary, beginning with the letter "A."
>
> Put an "x" in the right spot.
>
> The metal rod was shaped into a "V."

NOTE: Style varies on this point. Sans serif type is most often used when the shape of the letter is being stressed. Letters referred to as letters are commonly set in italic type. (For more on this use of italics, see the section on Other Uses of Italics, beginning on page 134, in Chapter 2, "Capitals, Italics, and Quotation Marks.") Finally, letters often appear in the same typeface as the surrounding text if no confusion would result from the styling.

> a V-shaped blade
>
> How many *e*'s are in her name?
>
> He was happy to get a B in the course.

With Other Marks of Punctuation

11. When quotation marks follow a word in a sentence that is also followed by a period or comma, the period or comma is placed within the quotation marks.

> He said, "I am leaving."
>
> Her camera was described as "waterproof," but "moisture-resistant" would have been a better description.

NOTE: Some writers draw a distinction between periods and commas that belong logically to the quoted material and those that belong to the whole sentence. If the period or comma belongs to the quoted material, they place it inside the quotation marks; if the period belongs logically to the sentence that surrounds the quoted matter, they place it outside the quotation marks. This distinction was previously observed in a wide range of publications, including U.S. Congressional publications and Merriam-Webster® dictionaries. In current practice, the distinction is made in relatively few publications, although the distinction is routinely made for dashes, exclamation points, and question marks used with quotation marks, as described in paragraph 13 below.

> The package was labeled "Handle with Care".
>
> The act was referred to as the "Army-Navy Medical Services Corps Act of 1947".
>
> Her camera was described as "waterproof", but "moisture-resistant" would have been a better description.
>
> He said, "I am leaving."

12. When quotation marks follow a word in a sentence that is also followed by a colon or semicolon, the colon or semicolon is placed outside the quotation marks.

> There was only one thing to do when he said, "I may not run": promise him a larger campaign contribution.
>
> She spoke of her "little cottage in the country"; she might better have called it a mansion.

13. The dash, question mark, and exclamation point are placed inside quotation marks when they punctuate the quoted matter only. They are placed outside the quotation marks when they punctuate the whole sentence.

> He asked, "When did she leave?"
>
> What is the meaning of "the open door"?
>
> Save us from his "mercy"!
>
> "I can't see how—" he started to say.
>
> He thought he knew where he was going—he remembered her saying, "Take two lefts, then stay to the right"—but the streets didn't look familiar.

14. One space follows a quotation mark that is followed by the rest of a sentence.

> "I am leaving," she said.

15. In typewritten material, two spaces follow a quotation mark that ends a sentence. In typeset material one space follows.

> He said, "Here is the car." I asked if I should get in.
>
> He said, "Here is the car." I asked if I should get in.

Quotation Marks, Single

1. Single quotation marks enclose a quotation within a quotation in conventional English.

The witness said, "I distinctly heard him say, 'Don't be late,' and then I heard the door close."

The witness said, "I distinctly heard him say, 'Don't be late.' "

NOTE: When both single and double quotation marks occur at the end of a sentence, the period typically falls *within* both sets of marks.

2. Single quotation marks are sometimes used in place of double quotation marks especially in British usage.

The witness said, 'I distinctly heard him say, "Don't be late," and then I heard the door close.'

3. On rare occasions, authors face the question of how to style a quotation within a quotation within a quotation. Standard styling practice would be to enclose the innermost quotation in double marks; however, this construction can be confusing, and in many cases rewriting the sentence can remove the need for it.

The witness said, "I distinctly heard him say, 'Don't you say "Shut up" to me.' "

The witness said that she distinctly heard him say, "Don't you say 'Shut up' to me."

4. In some specialized fields, such as theology, philosophy, and linguistics, special terminology or words referred to as words are enclosed within single quotation marks. When single quotation marks are used in this way, any other punctuation following

the word enclosed is placed outside the quotation marks.

> She was interested in the development of the word 'humongous', especially during the 1960s.

Semicolon

The semicolon is used in ways that are similar to those in which periods and commas are used. Because of these similarities, the semicolon is often thought of as either a weak period or a strong comma. As a weak period, the semicolon marks the end of a complete clause and signals that the clause that follows it is closely related to the clause that precedes it. As a strong comma, the semicolon clarifies meaning usually by distinguishing major sentence divisions from the minor pauses that are represented by commas.

Between Clauses

1. A semicolon separates independent clauses that are joined together in one sentence without a coordinating conjunction.

> He hemmed and hawed for over an hour; he couldn't make up his mind.
>
> The river rose and overflowed its banks; roads became flooded and impassable; freshly plowed fields disappeared from sight.
>
> Cream the shortening and sugar; add the eggs and beat well.

2. Ordinarily a comma separates main clauses joined with a coordinating conjunction. However, if the sentence might be confusing with a comma in this position, a semicolon is used in its place. Potentially confusing sentences include those with other commas in them or with particularly long clauses.

> We fear that this situation may, in fact, occur; but we don't know when.

> In a society that seeks to promote social goals, government will play a powerful role; and taxation, once simply a means of raising money, becomes, in addition, a way of furthering those goals.

> As recently as 1978 the company felt the operation could be a successful one that would generate significant profits in several different markets; but in 1981 the management changed its mind and began a program of shutting down plants and reducing its product line.

3. A semicolon joins two statements when the grammatical construction of the second clause is elliptical and depends on that of the first.

> The veal dishes were very good; the desserts, too.
> In many cases the conference sessions, which were designed to allow for full discussions of topics, were much too long and tedious; the breaks between them, much too short.

4. A semicolon joins two clauses when the second begins with a conjunctive adverb, as *accordingly, also, besides, consequently, furthermore, hence, however, indeed, likewise, moreover, namely, nevertheless, otherwise,*

still, then, therefore, and *thus.* Phrases such as *by the same token, in that case, as a result, on the other hand,* and *all the same* can also act as conjunctive adverbs.

> Most people are covered by insurance of one kind or another; indeed, many people don't even see their medical bills.
>
> It won't be easy to sort out the facts of this confusing situation; however, a decision must be made.
>
> The case could take years to work its way through the court system; as a result, many plaintiffs will accept out-of-court settlements.

NOTE: Style varies regarding the treatment of clauses introduced by *so* and *yet.* Although many writers continue to treat *so* and *yet* as adverbs, it has become standard to treat these words as coordinating conjunctions that join clauses. In this treatment, a comma precedes *so* and *yet* and no punctuation follows them. (For examples, see paragraph 1 under Comma in this chapter.)

5. When three or more clauses are separated by semicolons, a coordinating conjunction may or may not precede the final clause. If a coordinating conjunction does precede the final clause, the final semicolon is often replaced with a comma. (For the use of commas to separate three or more clauses without conjunctions, see paragraph 4 under Comma in this chapter.)

> Their report was one-sided and partial; it did not reflect the facts; it distorted them.
>
> They don't understand; they grow bored; and they stop learning.

The report recounted events leading up to the incident; it included observations of eyewitnesses, but it drew no conclusions.

NOTE: The choices of whether to use a conjunction and whether to use a semicolon or comma with the conjunction are matters of personal preference. In general, the force of the semicolon is to make the transition to the final clause more abrupt, which often serves to place more emphasis on that clause. The comma and conjunction ease the transition and make the sentence seem less choppy.

With Phrases and Clauses Introduced by *for example*, *i.e.*, etc.

6. A semicolon is sometimes used before expressions (as *for example, for instance, that is, namely, e.g.,* or *i.e.*) that introduce expansions or series. Commas, dashes, and parentheses are also used in sentences like these. For contrasting examples, see paragraph 18 under Comma, paragraph 6 under Dash, and paragraph 2 under Parentheses in this chapter.

On one point only did everyone agree; namely, that too much money had been spent already.

We were fairly successful on that project; that is, we made our deadlines and met our budget.

Most of the contestants had traveled great distances to participate; for example, three had come from Australia, one from Japan, and two from China.

In a Series

7. A semicolon is used in place of a comma to separate phrases in a series when the phrases them-

selves contain commas. A comma may replace the semicolon before the last item in a series if the last item is introduced with a conjunction.

> She flung open the door; raced up the stairs, taking them two at a time; locked herself in the bathroom; and, holding her sides, started to laugh uncontrollably.

> The visitor to Barndale was offered three sources of overnight accommodation: The Rose and Anchor, which housed Barndale's oldest pub; The Crawford, an American-style luxury hotel; and Ellen's Bed and Breakfast on Peabody Lane.

> We studied mathematics and geography in the morning; English, French, and Spanish right after lunch, and science in the late afternoon.

8. When the individual items in an enumeration or series are long or are sentences themselves, they are usually separated by semicolons.

> Among the committee's recommendations: more hospital beds in urban areas where there are waiting lists for elective surgery; smaller staff size in half-empty rural hospitals; review procedures for all major purchases.

> There is a difference between them: she is cross and irritable; he is merely moody.

As a Mechanical Device

9. A semicolon separates items in a list in cases where a comma alone would not clearly separate the items or references.

> (Friedlander 1957; Ballas 1962)
> (Genesis 3:1–19; 4:1–16)

With Other Marks of Punctuation

10. A semicolon is placed outside quotation marks and parentheses.

> They referred to each other as "Mother" and "Father"; they were the archetypal happily married elderly couple.

> She accepted the situation with every appearance of equanimity (but with some inward qualms); however, all of that changed the next day.

Virgule

The virgule is known by many names, including *diagonal, solidus, oblique, slant, slash,* and *slash mark*. Most commonly, the virgule is used to represent a word that is not written out or to separate or set off certain adjacent elements of text.

In Place of Missing Words

1. A virgule represents the word *per* or *to* when used with units of measure or when used to indicate the terms of a ratio.

> 40,000 tons/year
> 9 ft./sec.
> a 50/50 split
> 14 gm/100 cc
> price/earnings ratio
> risk/reward tradeoff

2. A virgule separates alternatives. In this context, the virgule usually represents the words *or* or *and/or*.

> alumni/ae
> his/her
> introductory/refresher courses
> oral/written tests

3. A virgule replaces the word *and* in some compound terms.

> molybdenum/vanadium steel
> in the May/June issue
> 1973/74
> in the Falls Church/McLean, Va., area
> an innovative classroom/laboratory

4. A virgule is used, although less commonly, to replace a number of prepositions, such as *at, versus, with,* and *for.*

> U.C./Berkeley
> parent/child issues
> table/mirror
> Vice President/Editorial

With Abbreviations

5. A virgule punctuates some abbreviations.

> c/o
> A/V
> d/b/a
> A/R
> A/1C
> S/Sgt
> w/
> V/STOL

NOTE: In some cases the virgule may stand for a word that is not represented in the abbreviation (e.g., *in* in *W/O,* the abbreviation for *water in oil*).

To Separate Elements

6. The virgule is used in a number of mechanical ways to separate groups of numbers, such as elements in a date, numerators and denominators in fractions, and area codes in telephone numbers. For more on the use of virgules with numbers, see Chapter 5, "The Treatment of Numbers."

7. The virgule serves as a divider between lines of poetry that are run in with the text around them. This method of quoting poetry is usually limited to passages of no more than three or four lines. Longer passages are usually set off from the text as extract quotations, with the lines set exactly as in the original, and without virgules separating them.

   When Samuel Taylor Coleridge wrote in "Christabel" that "'Tis a month before the month of May,/And the Spring comes slowly up this way," he could have been describing New England.

8. The virgule sets off certain elements—such as the parts of an address that are normally placed on separate lines—when they appear run in with the surrounding text.

   Mlle Christine Lagache/20, Passage des Écoliers/75051 Paris/France

9. The virgule sets off phonemes and phonemic transcriptions.

> /b/ as in *but*
> pronounced /ˌekə'nämik/ or /ˌēkə'nämik/

Spacing

10. In general, no space is used between the virgule and the words, letters, or figures separated by it. Some authors and editors prefer to place spaces around a virgule used to separate lines of poetry, but most omit the space. In the case of virgules used to set off phonemes and phonemic transcriptions, however, a space precedes the first virgule and follows the second virgule.

Chapter 2

Capitals, Italics, and Quotation Marks

CONTENTS

Words and phrases are capitalized, italicized, or enclosed in quotation marks in order to indicate that they have a special significance in a particular context. Some rules regarding capitals, italics, and quotation marks are backed by long tradition and are quite easy to apply ("The first word of a sentence or sentence fragment is capitalized"); others require arbitrary decisions or personal judgment ("Foreign words and phrases that have not been fully adopted into the English language are italicized"). Careful writers and editors usually make notes or keep a style sheet to record the decisions that they make so they can be consistent in their use of capitals, italics, and quotation marks.

This chapter is divided into four sections. The first section explains the use of capitalized words to begin sentences and phrases. The second section explains the use of capitals, italics, and quotation marks to indicate that a word or phrase is a proper noun, pronoun, or adjective. The third and fourth sections explain other uses of capital letters and italics. For other uses of quotation marks, see the section on Quotation Marks beginning on page 74, in Chapter 1, "Punctuation."

Beginnings

1. The first word of a sentence or sentence fragment is capitalized.

    > The meeting was postponed.
    > No! I cannot do it.
    > Will you go?
    > Total chaos. Nothing works.

2. The first word of a sentence contained within parentheses is capitalized; however, a parenthetical sentence occurring inside another sentence is not capitalized unless it is a complete quoted sentence.

    > The discussion was held in the boardroom. (The results are still confidential.)
    > Although we liked the restaurant (their Italian food was the best), we could not afford to eat there often.
    > After waiting in line for an hour (why do we do these things?), we finally left.
    > He was totally demoralized ("There is just nothing we can do") and was contemplating resignation.

3. The first word of a direct quotation is capitalized; however, if the quotation is interrupted in midsentence, the second part does not begin with a capital.

> The President said, "We have rejected this report entirely."
>
> "We have rejected this report entirely," the President said, "and we will not comment on it further."

4. When a quotation, whether a sentence fragment or a complete sentence, is syntactically dependent on the sentence in which it occurs, the quotation does not begin with a capital.

> The President made it clear that "there is no room for compromise."

5. The first word of a sentence within a sentence is usually capitalized. Examples of sentences within sentences include mottoes and rules, unspoken or imaginary dialogue, sentences referred to as sentences, and direct questions. (For an explanation of the use of commas and quotation marks with sentences such as these, see paragraphs 34 and 35 in the section on Comma, beginning on page 21, and paragraph 6 in the section on Quotation Marks, Double, beginning on page 74, in Chapter 1, "Punctuation."

> You know the saying, "A stitch in time saves nine."
> The first rule is, When in doubt, spell it out.
> The clear message coming back from the audience was "We don't care."
> My question is, When can we go?
> She kept wondering, how did they get here so soon?

NOTE: In the cases of unspoken or imaginary dialogue and of direct questions, it is a matter of individual preference whether or not to capitalize the first word; however, the most common practice is to capitalize it.

6. The first word of a line of poetry is conventionally capitalized.

> The best lack all conviction, while the worst
> Are full of passionate intensity.
> —W. B. Yeats

7. The first word following a colon may be either lowercased or capitalized if it introduces a complete sentence. While the former is the usual styling, the latter is also quite common, especially when the sentence introduced by the colon is fairly lengthy and distinctly separate from the preceding clause.

> The advantage of this particular system is clear: it's inexpensive.
> The situation is critical: This company cannot hope to recoup the fourth-quarter losses that were sustained in five operating divisions.

NOTE: For the sake of consistency, many authors and editors prefer to use one style or the other in all cases, regardless of sentence length. The capitalized style is more common in newspapers, but overall the lowercased styling is more frequently used.

8. If a colon introduces a series of sentences, the first word of each sentence is capitalized.

Consider the following steps that we have taken: A subcommittee has been formed to evaluate our past performance and to report its findings to the full organization. New sources of revenue are being explored, and relevant organizations are being contacted. And several candidates have been interviewed for the new post of executive director.

9. The first words of run-in enumerations that form complete sentences are capitalized, as are the first words of phrasal lists and enumerations arranged vertically beneath running texts. Phrasal enumerations run in with the introductory text, however, are lowercased.

   Do the following tasks at the end of the day: 1. Clean your typewriter. 2. Clear your desktop of papers. 3. Cover office machines. 4. Straighten the contents of your desk drawers, cabinets, and bookcases.

   This is the agenda:
   Call to order
   Roll call
   Minutes of the previous meeting
   Treasurer's report

   On the agenda will be (1) call to order, (2) roll call, (3) minutes of the previous meeting, (4) treasurer's report . . .

10. The introductory words *Whereas* and *Resolved* are capitalized in minutes and legislation, as is the word *That* or an alternative word or expression which immediately follows either.

   Resolved, That . . .
   Whereas, Substantial benefits . . .

11. The first word in an outline heading is capitalized.

> I. Editorial tasks
> II. Production responsibilities
> A. Cost estimates
> B. Bids

12. The first word of the salutation of a letter and the first word of a complimentary close are capitalized.

> Dear Mary,
> Dear Sir or Madam:
> Ladies and Gentlemen:
> Gentlemen:
> Sincerely yours,
> Very truly yours,

13. The first word and each subsequent major word following a SUBJECT or TO heading (as in a memorandum) are capitalized.

> SUBJECT: Pension Plans
> TO: All Department Heads and Editors

Proper Nouns, Pronouns, and Adjectives

This section describes the ways in which a broad range of proper nouns, pronouns, and adjectives are styled—with capitals, italics, quotation marks, or some combination of these devices. In almost all cases, proper nouns, pronouns, and adjectives are capitalized. The essential distinction in the use of capitals and lowercase letters lies in the particularizing or individualizing significance of capitals as against the generalizing significance of lowercase. A capital is used with a proper noun because it distinguishes some individual person, place, or thing from others of the same class. A capital is used with a proper adjective because it takes its descriptive meaning from a proper noun.

In many cases, proper nouns are italicized or enclosed in quotation marks in addition to being capitalized. No clear distinctions can be drawn between the kinds of words that are capitalized and italicized, capitalized and enclosed in quotation marks, or simply capitalized, as styling on these points is governed almost wholly by tradition.

The paragraphs in this section are grouped under the following alphabetically arranged headings:

Abbreviations
Abstractions and Personifications
Academic Degrees
Animals and Plants
Awards, Honors, and Prizes
Derivatives of Proper Names
Geographical and Topographical References
Governmental, Judicial, and Political Bodies
Historical Periods and Events
Hyphenated Compounds
Legal Material
Medical Terms
Military Terms
Numerical Designations
Organizations
People
Pronouns

Religious Terms
Scientific Terms
Time Periods and Zones
Titles
Trademarks
Transportation

Abbreviations

1. Abbreviated forms of proper nouns and adjectives are capitalized, just as the spelled-out forms would be. For more on the capitalization of abbreviations, see the section on Capitalization, beginning on page 190, in Chapter 4, "Abbreviations."

Dec. for *December*
Wed. for *Wednesday*
Col. for *Colonel*
Brit. for *British*

Abstractions and Personifications

2. Abstract terms, such as names of concepts or qualities, are usually not capitalized unless the concept or quality is being presented as if it were a person. If the term is simply being used in conjunction with other words that allude to human characteristics or qualities, it is usually not capitalized. For more on the capitalization of abstract terms, see the section on Other Uses of Capitals in this chapter.

a time when Peace walked among us
as Autumn paints each leaf in fiery colors
an economy gripped by inflation
hoping that fate would lend a hand

3. Fictitious names used as personifications are capitalized.

> Uncle Sam
> Ma Bell
> John Bull
> Jack Frost
> Big Oil squirmed under the new regulations.

Academic Degrees

4. The names of academic degrees are capitalized when they follow a person's name. The names of specific academic degrees not following a person's name are capitalized or not capitalized according to individual preference. General terms referring to degrees, such as *doctorate, master's degree,* or *bachelor's* are not capitalized. Abbreviations for academic degrees are always capitalized.

> Martin Bonkowski, Doctor of Divinity
> earned her Doctor of Laws degree *or* earned her doctor of laws degree
> working for a bachelor's degree
> Susan Wycliff, M.S.W.
> received her Ph.D.

Animals and Plants

5. The common names of animals and plants are not capitalized unless they contain a proper noun as a separate element, in which case the proper noun is capitalized, but any element of the name following the proper noun is lowercased. Elements of the

name preceding the proper noun are usually but not always capitalized. In some cases, the common name of the plant or animal contains a word that was once a proper noun but is no longer thought of as such. In these cases, the word is usually not capitalized. When in doubt about the capitalization of a plant or animal name, consult a dictionary. (For an explanation of the capitalization of genus names in binomial nomenclature or of New Latin names for groups above genera in zoology and botany, see paragraphs 67 and 68 below.)

> cocker spaniel
> lily of the valley
> ponderosa pine
> great white shark
> Hampshire hog
> Kentucky bluegrass
> Steller's jay
> Bengal tiger
> Japanese beetle
> Rhode Island red
> Great Dane
> Brown Swiss
> black-eyed Susan
> wandering Jew
> holstein

NOTE: In references to specific breeds, as distinguished from the animals that belong to the breed, all elements of the name are capitalized.

> Gordon Setter
> Rhode Island Red
> Holstein

Awards, Honors, and Prizes

6. Names of awards, honors, and prizes are capitalized. Descriptive words and phrases that are not actually part of the award's name are lowercased. (For an explanation of capitalizing the names of military decorations, see paragraph 44 below.)

> Academy Award
> Emmy
> New York Drama Critics' Circle Award
> Nobel Prize
> Nobel Prize in medicine
> Nobel Prize winner
> Nobel Peace Prize
> Rhodes Scholarship
> Rhodes scholar

Brand Names—See **Trademarks** below.

Computer Terms—See **Scientific Terms** below.

Derivatives of Proper Names

7. Derivatives of proper names are capitalized when they are used in their primary sense. However, if the derived term has taken on a specialized meaning, it is usually not capitalized.

> Roman architecture
> Victorian customs
> Keynesian economics
> an Americanism
> an Egyptologist
> french fries

manila envelope
pasteurized milk
a quixotic undertaking

Geographical and Topographical References

8. Terms that identify divisions of the earth's surface
    and distinct areas, regions, places, or districts are
    capitalized, as are derivative nouns and adjectives.

    Chicago, Illinois
    Tropic of Capricorn
    the Middle Eastern situation
    the Western Hemisphere
    the Southwest
    the Sunbelt

9. Popular names of localities are capitalized.

    the Big Apple
    the Loop
    Hell's Kitchen
    the Village
    the Twin Cities
    the Valley

10. Compass points are capitalized when they refer to
    a geographical region or when they are part of a
    street name. They are lowercased when they refer to
    a simple direction.

    back East
    West Columbus Avenue
    up North
    South Pleasant Street
    out West
    down South

> east of the Mississippi
> traveling north on I-91

11. Nouns and adjectives that are derived from compass points and that designate or refer to a specific geographical region are usually capitalized.

> a Southern accent
> a Western crop
> Northerners
> part of the Eastern establishment

12. Words designating global, national, regional, or local political divisions are capitalized when they are essential elements of specific names. However, they are usually lowercased when they precede a proper name or when they are not part of a specific name.

> the British Empire
> New York City
> Washington State
> Ward 1
> Hampden County
> Ohio's Ninth Congressional District
> the fall of the empire
> the city of New York
> the state of Washington
> fires in three wards
> the county of Hampden
> carried her district

NOTE: In legal documents, these words are often capitalized regardless of position.

> the State of Washington
> the County of Hampden
> the City of New York

13. Generic geographical terms (as *lake, mountain, river, valley*) are capitalized if they are part of a specific proper name.

> Crater Lake
> Lake Como
> Rocky Mountains
> the Columbia River
> Ohio Valley
> Long Island
> Great Barrier Reef
> Atlantic Ocean
> Niagara Falls
> Hudson Bay
> Strait of Gibraltar
> Bering Strait

14. Generic geographical terms preceding names are usually capitalized.

> Lakes Mead and Powell
> Mounts Whitney and Shasta

NOTE: When *the* precedes the generic term, the generic term is lowercased.

> the river Thames

15. Generic geographical terms that are not used as part of a proper name are not capitalized. These include plural generic geographical terms that follow two or more proper names and generic terms that are used descriptively or alone.

> the Himalaya and Andes mountains
> the Missouri and Platte rivers
> the Atlantic coast of Labrador

the Arizona desert
the Mississippi delta
the Caribbean islands
the river valley
the valley

16. The names of streets, monuments, parks, land-marks, well-known buildings, and other public places are capitalized. However, generic terms that are part of these names (as *avenue, bridge,* or *tower*) are lowercased when they occur after multiple names or are used alone (but see paragraph 17 below).

> Golden Gate Bridge
> the Capitol
> Rock Creek Park
> Eddystone Lighthouse
> the Dorset Hotel
> Fanueil Hall
> the San Diego Zoo
> Coit Tower
> the Mall
> the Pyramids
> the Statue of Liberty
> Peachtree Street
> the Dorset and Drake hotels
> Fifth and Park avenues
> on the bridge
> walking through the park

17. Well-known informal or shortened forms of place-names are capitalized.

> the Avenue for *Fifth Avenue*
> the Street for *Wall Street*
> the Exchange for the *New York Stock Exchange*

Governmental, Judicial, and Political Bodies

18. Full names of legislative, deliberative, executive, and administrative bodies are capitalized, as are easily recognizable short forms of these names. However, nonspecific noun and adjective references to them are usually lowercased.

> United States Congress
> the Federal Reserve Board
> the Congress
> the House
> the Federal Bureau of Investigation
> the Fed
> congressional hearings
> a federal agency

NOTE: Style varies regarding the capitalization of words such as *department, committee,* or *agency* when they are being used in place of the full name of a specific body. They are most often capitalized when the department or agency is referring to itself in print. In most other cases, these words are lowercased.

> The Connecticut Department of Transportation is pleased to offer this new booklet on traffic safety. The Department hopes that it will be of use to all drivers.

> We received a new booklet from the Connecticut Department of Transportation. This is the second pamphlet the department has issued this month.

19. The U.S. Supreme Court and the short forms *Supreme Court* and *Court* referring to it are capitalized.

> the Supreme Court of the United States
> the United States Supreme Court

the Supreme Court
the Court

20. Official and full names of higher courts and names of international courts are capitalized. Short forms of official higher court names are often capitalized in legal documents but lowercased in general writing.

> The International Court of Arbitration
> the United States Court of Appeals for the Second Circuit
> the Virginia Supreme Court
> the Court of Queen's Bench
> a ruling by the court of appeals
> the state supreme court

21. Names of city and county courts are usually lowercased.

> the Lawton municipal court
> police court
> the Owensville night court
> the county court
> small claims court
> juvenile court

22. The single designation *court,* when specifically applicable to a judge or a presiding officer, is capitalized.

> It is the opinion of this Court that . . .
> The Court found that . . .

23. The terms *federal* and *national* are capitalized only when they are essential elements of a name or title.

Federal Trade Commission
National Security Council
federal court
national security

24. The word *administration* is capitalized in some publications when it refers to the administration of a specific United States president; however, the word is more commonly lowercased in this situation. If the word does not refer to a specific presidential administration, it is not capitalized except when it is a part of an official name of a government agency.

the Truman administration *or* the Truman Administration
the administration *or* the Administration
the Farmers Home Loan Administration

The running of the White House varies considerably from one administration to another.

25. Names of political organizations and their adherents are capitalized, but the word *party* may or may not be capitalized, depending on the writer's or publication's preference.

the Democratic National Committee
the Republican platform
Tories
Nazis
the Democratic party *or* the Democratic Party
the Communist party *or* the Communist Party

26. Names of political groups other than parties are usually lowercased, as are their derivative forms.

rightist
right wing
left winger
but usually
the Left
the Right

27. Terms describing political and economic philosophies and their derivative forms are usually capitalized only if they are derived from proper names.

authoritarianism
nationalism
isolationist
democracy
supply-side economics
civil libertarian
fascism   *or*   Fascism
social Darwinism
Marxist

Historical Periods and Events

28. The names of conferences, councils, expositions, and specific sporting, historical, and cultural events are capitalized.

the Yalta Conference
the Congress of Vienna
the Minnesota State Fair
the Games of the XXIII Olympiad
the World Series
the Series
the Boston Tea Party
the San Francisco Earthquake
the Bonus March of 1932
the Philadelphia Folk Festival
the Golden Gate International Exposition

29. The names of some historical and cultural periods and movements are capitalized. When in doubt about such a name, consult a dictionary or encyclopedia.

> Augustan Age
> Renaissance
> Stone Age
> Prohibition
> the Enlightenment
> the Great Depression
> fin de siècle
> space age
> cold war *or* Cold War

30. Numerical designations of historical time periods are capitalized only when they are part of a proper name; otherwise they are lowercased.

> the Third Reich
> Roaring Twenties
> seventeenth century
> eighties

31. Full names of treaties, laws, and acts are capitalized.

> Treaty of Versailles
> The Controlled Substances Act of 1970

32. The full names of wars are capitalized; however, words such as *war, revolution, battle,* and *campaign* are capitalized only when they are part of a proper name. Descriptive terms such as *assault, seige,* and *engagement* are usually lowercased even when used

in conjunction with the name of the place where
the action occurred.

> the French and Indian War
> the Spanish American War
> the War of the Roses
> the Six-Day War
> the War of the Spanish Succession
> the American Revolution
> the Whiskey Rebellion
> the Revolution of 1688
> the Battle of the Coral Sea
> the Battle of the Bulge
> the naval battle of Guadalcanal
> the Peninsular Campaign
> the American and French revolutions
> the second battle of Manassas
> the seige of Yorktown
> the Meuse-Argonne offensive
> the winter campaign
> the assault on Iwo Jima
> was in action throughout most of the war

Hyphenated Compounds

33. Elements of hyphenated compounds are capital-
    ized if they are proper nouns or adjectives.

> Arab-Israeli negotiations
> Tay-Sachs disease
> East-West trade agreements
> U.S.-U.S.S.R. détente
> an eighteenth-century poet
> American-plan rates

NOTE: If the second element in a two-word compound is not a proper noun or adjective, it is lowercased.

French-speaking peoples
an A-frame house
Thirty-second Street

34. Word elements (as prefixes and combining forms) may or may not be capitalized when joined to a proper noun or adjective. Common prefixes (as *pre-* or *anti-*) are usually not capitalized when so attached. Geographical and ethnic combining forms (as *Anglo-* or *Afro-*) are capitalized; *pan-* is usually capitalized when attached to a proper noun or adjective.

the pro-Soviet faction
post–Civil War politics
un-American activities
Afro-Americans
Sino-Soviet relations
Greco-Roman architecture
Pan-Slavic nationalism
the Pan-African Congress

Languages—See **People** below.

Legal Material—See also **Governmental, Judicial, and Political Bodies** above.

35. The names of both plaintiff and defendant in legal case titles are italicized. The *v.* for *versus* may be roman or italic. Cases that do not involve two opposing parties have titles such as *In re Watson* or *In the matter of John Watson*; these case titles are also italicized. When the person involved rather than the case itself is being discussed, the reference is not italicized.

Jones v. *Massachusetts*
In re Jones
Smith et al. v. Jones
She covered the Jones trial for the newspaper.

NOTE: In running text a case name involving two opposing parties may be shortened.

The judge based his ruling on a precedent set in the *Jones* decision.

Medical Terms

36. Proper names that are elements in terms designating diseases, symptoms, syndromes, and tests are capitalized. Common nouns are lowercased.

Down's syndrome
Parkinson's disease
Duchenne-Erb paralysis
Rorschach test
German measles
syndrome of Weber
acquired immunodeficiency syndrome
mumps
measles
herpes simplex

37. Taxonomic names of disease-causing organisms follow the rules established for binomial nomenclature discussed in paragraph 67 below. The names of diseases or pathological conditions derived from taxonomic names of organisms are lowercased and not italicized.

a neurotoxin produced by *Clostridium botulinum*
nearly died of botulism

38. Generic names of drugs are lowercased; trade names should be capitalized.

> a prescription for chlorpromazine
> had been taking Thorazine

Military Terms

39. The full titles of branches of the armed forces are capitalized, as are easily recognized short forms of full branch designations.

> U.S. Air Force
> the Air Force
> U.S. Navy
> the Navy
> U.S. Army
> the Army
> U.S. Coast Guard
> the Coast Guard
> U.S. Marine Corps
> the Marine Corps
> the Marines
> the Corps

40. The terms *air force, army, coast guard, marine(s),* and *navy* are lowercased unless they form a part of an official name or refer back to a specific branch of the armed forces previously named. They are also lowercased when they are used collectively or in the plural.

> the combined air forces of the NATO nations
> the navies of the world
> the American army
>
> In some countries the duty of the coast guard may include icebreaking in inland waterways.

41. The adjectives *naval* and *marine* are lowercased unless they are part of a proper name.

> naval battle
> marine barracks
> Naval Reserves

42. The full titles of units and organizations of the armed forces are capitalized. Elements of full titles are lowercased when they stand alone.

> U.S. Army Corps of Engineers
> the corps
> the Reserves
> a reserve commission
> First Battalion
> the battalion
> 4th Marine Regiment
> the regiment
> Eighth Fleet
> the fleet
> Cruiser Division
> the division
> Fifth Army
> the army

43. Military ranks are capitalized when they precede the names of their holders, and when they take the place of a person's name (as in direct address). Otherwise they are lowercased.

> Admiral Nimitz
> General Creighton W. Abrams
> I can't get this rifle any cleaner, Sergeant.
> The major arrived precisely on time.

44. The specific names of decorations, citations, and medals are capitalized.

> Medal of Honor
> Purple Heart
> Silver Star
> Navy Cross
> Distinguished Service Medal

Nicknames—See paragraphs 49, 51, and 52 below.

Numerical Designations

45. A noun introducing a reference number is usually capitalized.

> Order 704
> Flight 409
> Form 2E
> Policy 118-4-Y

46. Nouns used with numbers or letters to designate major reference headings (as in a literary work) are capitalized. However, nouns designating minor reference headings are typically lowercased.

> Book II
> Table 3
> paragraph 6.1
> Volume V
> page 101
> item 16
> Division 4
> line 8
> question 21
> Figure 1
> note 10

Organizations

47. Names of firms, corporations, schools, and organizations and terms derived from those names to designate their members are capitalized. However, common nouns used descriptively or occurring after the names of two or more organizations are lowercased.

> Merriam-Webster Inc.
> Rotary International
> University of Michigan
> Kiwanians
> Smith College
> American and United airlines
> Washington Huskies
> Minnesota North Stars
> played as a Pirate last year

NOTE: The word *the* at the beginning of such names is capitalized only when the full legal name is used.

48. Words such as *agency, department, division, group,* or *office* that designate corporate and organizational units are capitalized only when they are used with a specific name.

> while working for the Criminal Division in the Department of Justice
> a notice to all department heads

NOTE: Style varies regarding the capitalization of these words when they are used in place of the full name of a specific body. For more on this aspect of styling, see the note following paragraph 18 above.

49. Nicknames, epithets, or other alternate terms for organizations are capitalized.

> referred to IBM as Big Blue
> the Big Three automakers
> trading stocks on the Big Board

People

50. The names and initials of persons are capitalized. If a name is hyphenated, both elements are capitalized. Particles forming the initial elements of surnames (as *de, della, der, du, la, ten, ter, van,* and *von*) may or may not be capitalized, depending on the styling of the individual name. However, if a name with a lowercase initial particle begins a sentence, the particle is capitalized.

> Thomas de Quincey
> E. I. du Pont de Nemours
> Sir Arthur Thomas Quiller-Couch
> Gerald ter Hoerst
> James Van Allen
> Heinrich Wilhelm Von Kleist
> the paintings of de Kooning
> De Kooning's paintings are . . .

51. The name of a person or thing can be added to or replaced entirely by a nickname or epithet, a characterizing word or phrase. Nicknames and epithets are capitalized.

> Calamity Jane
> the Golden Bear
> Doctor J.
> Buffalo Bill

Wilt the Stilt
Attila the Hun
Louis the Fat
Murph the Surf
Dizzy Gillespie
Bubba Smith
Dusty Rhodes
Rusty Staub
Goose Gossage
Bird Parker
Meadowlark Lemon
Big Mama Thornton
Night Train Lane
Lefty Grove

52. Nicknames and epithets are frequently used in conjunction with both the first and last names of a person. If the nickname or epithet is placed between the first and last name, it will often be enclosed in quotation marks or parentheses; however, if the nickname is expected to be very well known to readers, the quotation marks or parentheses are often omitted. If the nickname precedes the first name, it is sometimes enclosed in quotation marks, but more often it is not.

Thomas P. "Tip" O'Neill
Joanne "Big Mama" Carner
Earl ("Fatha") Hines
Dennis (Oil Can) Boyd
Mary Harris ("Mother") Jones
Anna Mary Robertson "Grandma" Moses
Kissin' Jim Folsom
Blind Lemon Jefferson
Slammin' Sammy Snead
Mother Maybelle Carter

53. Words of family relationship preceding or used in place of a person's name are capitalized. However, these words are lowercased if they are part of a noun phrase that is being used in place of a name.

> Cousin Mercy
> Grandfather Barnes
> I know when Mother's birthday is.
> I know when my mother's birthday is.

54. Words designating languages, nationalities, peoples, races, religious groups, and tribes are capitalized. Descriptive terms used to refer to groups of people are variously capitalized or lowercased. Designations based on color are usually lowercased.

> Latin
> Canadians
> Ibo
> Afro-American
> Caucasians
> Muslims
> Christians
> Navajo
> Bushman (for a nomadic hunter of southern Africa)
> bushman (for an inhabitant of the Australian bush)
> the red man in America
> black, brown, and white people

55. Corporate, professional, and governmental titles are capitalized when they immediately precede a person's name, unless the name is being used as an appositive.

> President Roosevelt
> Queen Elizabeth

Senator Henry Jackson
Doctor Malatesta
Professor Greenbaum
Pastor Linda Jones

They wanted to meet the new pastor, Linda Jones.

Almost everyone has heard of Chrysler's president, Lee Iacocca.

56. When corporate or governmental titles are used as part of a descriptive phrase to identify a person rather than as a person's official title, the title is lowercased.

Senator Ted Stevens of Alaska *but* Ted Stevens, senator from Alaska
Lee Iacocca, president of Chrysler Corporation

NOTE: Style varies when governmental titles are used in descriptive phrases that precede a name.

Alaska senator Ted Stevens *or* Alaska Senator Ted Stevens

57. Specific governmental titles may be capitalized when they are used in place of particular individuals' names. In minutes and official records of proceedings, corporate titles are capitalized when they are used in place of individuals' names.

The Secretary of State gave a news conference.
The Judge will respond to questions in her chambers.
The Treasurer then stated his misgivings about the project.

58. Some publications always capitalize the word *president* when it refers to the United States presidency.

However, the more common practice is to capitalize the word *president* only when it refers to a specific individual.

> It is one of the duties of the President to submit a budget to Congress.
> It is one of the duties of the president to submit a budget to Congress.

59. Titles are capitalized when they are used in direct address.

> Tell me the truth, Doctor.
> Where are we headed, Captain?

Personifications—See Abstractions and Personifications above.

Prefixes—See Hyphenated Compounds above.

Pronouns

60. The pronoun *I* is capitalized. For pronouns referring to the Deity, see rule 62 below.

> He and I will attend the meeting.

Religious Terms

61. Words designating the Deity are capitalized.

> Allah
> God Almighty
> Christ
> Jehovah
> Yahweh
> the Holy Spirit

62. Personal pronouns referring to the Deity are usually capitalized. Relative pronouns (as *who, whom,* and *whose*) usually are not.

> God in His mercy
> when God asks us to do His bidding
> believing that it was God who created the universe

NOTE: Some style manuals maintain that the pronoun does not need to be capitalized if it is closely preceded by its antecedent; however, in current practice, most writers capitalize the pronoun regardless of its position.

63. Traditional designations of apostles, prophets, and saints are capitalized.

> our Lady
> the Prophet
> the Lawgiver

64. Names of religions, denominations, creeds and confessions, and religious orders are capitalized, as are adjectives derived from these names. The word *church* is capitalized only when it is used as part of the name of a specific body or edifice or, in some publications, when it refers to organized Christianity in general.

> Judaism
> Catholicism
> the Church of Christ
> the Southern Baptist Convention
> Apostles' Creed
> the Society of Jesus
> the Poor Clares
> Franciscans

Hunt Memorial Church
a Buddhist monastery
Islamic
the Baptist church on the corner
the Thirty-nine Articles of the Church of England

65. Names of the Bible or its books, parts, versions, or editions of it and other sacred books are capitalized but not italicized. Adjectives derived from the names of sacred books are variously capitalized and lowercased. When in doubt, consult a dictionary.

Authorized Version
Old Testament
Apocrypha
Talmud
Genesis
Pentateuch
Gospel of Saint Mark
Koran
biblical
talmudic
Koranic
Vedic

66. The names of prayers and well-known passages of the Bible are capitalized.

Ave Maria
the Sermon on the Mount
Ten Commandments
the Beatitudes
the Lord's Prayer
the Our Father

Scientific Terms

67. Genus names in biological binomial nomenclature are capitalized; species names are lowercased, even when derived from a proper name. Both genus and species names are italicized.

> Both the wolf and the domestic dog are included in the genus *Canis*.
>
> The California condor (*Gymnogyps californianus*) is facing extinction.
>
> Trailing arbutus (*Epigaea repens*) and rue anemone (*Anemonella thalictroides*) are among the earliest wildflowers to bloom in the spring.

NOTE: When used, the names of races, varieties, or subspecies are lowercased. Like genus and species names, they are italicized.

> *Hyla versicolor chrysoscelis*
> *Otis asio naevius*

68. The New Latin names of classes, families, and all groups above the genus level in zoology and botany are capitalized but not italicized. Their derivative adjectives and nouns in English are neither capitalized nor italicized.

> Gastropoda
> gastropod
> Thallophyta
> thallophyte

69. The names, both scientific and informal, of planets and their satellites, asteroids, stars, constellations, groups of stars, and other unique celestial objects are capitalized. However, the words *sun, earth,* and *moon* are usually lowercased unless they occur with other astronomical names. Generic terms that are the final element in the name of a celestial object are usually lowercased.

Ganymede
Sirius
Great Bear
the Milky Way
Venus
Ursa Major
Pleiades
Big Dipper
Barnard's star
probes heading for the Moon and Mars

70. Names of meteorological phenomena are lowercased.

aurora australis
northern lights
aurora borealis
parhelic circle

71. Terms that identify geological eras, periods, epochs, and strata are capitalized. The generic terms that follow them are lowercased. The words *upper, middle,* and *lower* are capitalized when they are used to designate an epoch or series within a period; in most other cases, they are lowercased. The word *age* is capitalized in names such as *Age of Reptiles* or *Age of Fishes.*

Mesozoic era
Quaternary period

Oligocene epoch
Upper Cretaceous
Middle Ordovician
Lower Silurian

72. Proper names forming essential elements of scientific laws, theorems, and principles are capitalized. However, the common nouns *law, theorem, theory,* and the like are lowercased.

Boyle's law
Planck's constant
the Pythagorean theorem
Einstein's theory of relativity

NOTE: In terms referring to popular or fanciful theories or observations, descriptive words are usually capitalized as well.

Murphy's Law
the Peter Principle

73. The names of chemical elements and compounds are lowercased.

hydrogen fluoride
ferric ammonium citrate

74. The names of computer services and data bases are usually trademarks and should always be capitalized. The names of computer languages are irregularly styled either with an initial capital letter or with all letters capitalized. The names of some computer languages are commonly written either way. When in doubt, consult a dictionary.

CompuServe
TeleTransfer
Dow Jones News Retrieval Service
Atek
Pascal
BASIC
COBOL *or* Cobol
APL
PENTA
PL/1
FORTRAN *or* Fortran

Time Periods and Zones

75. The names of days of the week, months of the
year, and holidays and holy days are capitalized.

Easter
Independence Day
June
Passover
Memorial Day
Thanksgiving
Tuesday
Yom Kippur
Ramadan

76. The names of time zones are capitalized when abbreviated but usually lowercased when written out
except for words that are themselves proper
names.

CST
central standard time
mountain time
Pacific standard time

77. Names of the seasons are lowercased if they simply declare the time of year; however, they are capitalized if they are personified.

> My new book is scheduled to appear this spring.
> the sweet breath of Spring

Titles—For titles of people, see **People** above.

78. Words in titles of books, long poems, magazines, newspapers, plays, movies, novellas that are separately published, and works of art such as paintings and sculpture are capitalized except for internal articles, conjunctions, prepositions, and the *to* of infinitives. The entire title is italicized. For the styling of the Bible and other sacred works, see paragraph 65 above.

> *The Lives of a Cell*
> *Of Mice and Men*
> *Saturday Review*
> *Christian Science Monitor*
> Shakespeare's *Othello*
> *The Old Man and the Sea*
> Gainsborough's *Blue Boy*
> the movie *Wait until Dark*

NOTE: Some publications also capitalize prepositions of five or more letters (as *about* or *toward*).

79. An initial article that is part of a title is often omitted if it would be awkward in context. However, when it is included it is capitalized and italicized. A common exception to this style regards books that are referred to by an abbreviation. In this case, the initial article is neither capitalized nor italicized.

> *The Oxford English Dictionary*
> the 13-volume *Oxford English Dictionary*
> the *OED*

80. Style varies widely regarding the capitalization and italicization of initial articles and city names in the titles of newspapers. One style rule that can be followed is to capitalize and italicize any word that is part of the official title of the paper as shown on its masthead. However, this information is not always available, and even if it is available it can lead to apparent inconsistencies in styling. Because of this, many publications choose one way of styling newspaper titles regardless of their official titles. The most common styling is to italicize the city name but not to capitalize or italicize the initial article.

> the *New York Times*
> the *Wall Street Journal*
> the *Des Moines Register*
> the *Washington Post*

81. Many publications, especially newspapers, do not use italics to style titles. They either simply capitalize the words of the title or capitalize the words and enclose them in quotation marks.

> the Heard on the Street column in the Wall Street Journal
> our review of "The Lives of a Cell" in last week's column

82. The first word following a colon in a title is capitalized.

> John Crowe Ransom: An Annotated Bibliography

83. The titles of short poems, short stories, essays, lectures, dissertations, chapters of books, articles in periodicals, radio and television programs, and novellas that are published in a collection are capitalized and enclosed in quotation marks. The capitalization of articles, conjunctions, and prepositions is the same as it is for italicized titles, as explained in paragraph 78 above.

> Robert Frost's "Dust of Snow"
>
> Katherine Anne Porter's "That Tree"
>
> John Barth's "The Literature of Exhaustion"
>
> The talk, "Labor's Power: A View for the Eighties," will be given next week.
>
> the third chapter of *Treasure Island,* entitled "The Black Spot"
>
> Her article, "Computer Art on a Micro," was in last month's *Popular Computing.*
>
> listening to "A Prairie Home Companion"
>
> watching "The Tonight Show"
>
> D. H. Lawrence's "The Woman Who Rode Away"

84. Common titles of sections of books (as a preface, introduction, or index) are capitalized but not enclosed in quotation marks when they refer to a section of the same book in which the reference is made. If they refer to another book, they are usually lowercased.

> See the Appendix for further information.
>
> In the introduction to her book, the author explains her goals.

85. Style varies regarding the capitalization of the word
chapter when it is used with a cardinal number to
identify a specific chapter in a book. In some publications the word is lowercased, but more commonly
it is capitalized.

> See Chapter 3 for more details.
> is discussed further in Chapter Four
>   *but*   in the third chapter

86. The titles of long musical compositions such as op-
eras and symphonies are capitalized and italicized;
the titles of short compositions are capitalized and
enclosed in quotation marks. The titles of musical
compositions identified by the nature of the musical form in which they were written are capitalized
only.

> Verdi's *Don Carlos*
> "America the Beautiful"
> Ravel's "Bolero"
> Serenade No. 12 in C Minor

Trademarks

87. Registered trademarks, service marks, collective
marks, and brand names are capitalized.

> Band-Aid
> Jacuzzi
> Kleenex
> Grammy
> Realtor
> Kellogg's All-Bran
> Diet Pepsi
> Lay's potato chips

Transportation

88. The names of individual ships, submarines, airplanes, satellites, and space vehicles are capitalized and italicized. The designations *U.S.S., S.S., M.V.,* and *H.M.S.* are not italicized.

> *Apollo 11*
> *Enola Gay*
> *Mariner 5*
> *Explorer 10*
> *Spirit of Saint Louis*
> M.V. *West Star*

Other Uses of Capitals

1. Full capitalization of a word is sometimes used for emphasis or to indicate that a speaker is talking very loudly. Both of these uses of capitals are usually avoided or at least used very sparingly in formal prose. Italicization of words for emphasis is more common. For examples of this use of italics, see paragraph 8 of the section on Other Uses of Italics in this chapter.

> Results are not the only criteria for judging performance. HOW we achieve results is important also.

> All applications must be submitted IN WRITING before January 31.

> The waiter rushed by yelling "HOT PLATE! HOT PLATE!"

2. A word is sometimes capitalized to indicate that it is being used as a philosophical concept or to indicate that it stands for an important concept in a discussion. Style manuals generally discourage this practice, but it is still in common use today even in formal writing.

> Many people seek Truth, but few find it.
>
> the three M's of advertising, Message, Media, and Management

3. Full capitals or a mixture of capitals and lowercase letters or sometimes even small capitals are used to reproduce the text of signs, labels, or inscriptions.

> a poster reading SPECIAL THRILLS COMING SOON
> a Do Not Disturb sign
> a barn with CHEW MAIL POUCH on the side
> a truck with WASH ME written in the dust

4. A letter used to indicate a shape is usually capitalized. If sans serif type is available, it is often used for such a letter, because it usually best approximates the shape that is being referred to.

> an A-frame house
> a J-bar
> V-shaped

Other Uses of Italics

Italic type is used to indicate that there is something out of the ordinary about a word or phrase or about the way in which it is being used. For some of the uses listed below, quotation marks can be substituted. For more on this use of quotation marks, see the section on Quotation Marks, Double, in Chapter 1, "Punctuation," beginning on page 74. For each of the uses listed below, underlining is used in place of italicizing when the text is typewritten instead of typeset.

1. Foreign words and phrases that have not been fully adopted into the English language are italicized. The decision whether or not to italicize a word will vary according to the context of the writing and the audience for which the writing is intended. In general, however, any word that appears in the main A–Z vocabulary section of *Webster's Ninth New Collegiate Dictionary* does not need to be italicized.

    > These accomplishments will serve as a monument, *aere perennius,* to the group's skill and dedication.
    >
    > They looked upon this area as a *cordon sanitaire* around the city.
    >
    > "The cooking here is *wunderbar,*" he said.
    >
    > After the concert, the crowd headed en masse for the parking lot.
    >
    > The committee meets on an ad hoc basis.

    NOTE: A complete sentence (such as a motto) can also be italicized. However, passages that comprise more than one sentence, or even a single sentence if it is particularly long, are usually treated as quotations; i.e., they are set in roman type and enclosed in quotation marks.

2. Unfamiliar words or words that have a specialized meaning are set in italics, especially when they are accompanied by a short definition. Once these

words have been introduced and defined, they do not need to be italicized in subsequent references.

> *Vitiligo* is a condition in which skin pigment cells stop making pigment.

> Another method is the *direct-to-consumer* transaction in which the publisher markets directly to the individual by mail or door-to-door.

3. Style varies somewhat regarding the italicization of Latin abbreviations. During the first half of this century, these abbreviations were most commonly set in italic type. Some authors and publishers still italicize them, either by tradition or on the grounds that they should be treated like foreign words. However, most authors and publishers now set these abbreviations in roman type. (For an explanation of the use of *ibid., op. cit.,* and other Latin bibliographical abbreviations, see Chapter 6, "Notes and Bibliographies.")

   et al.   cf.   e.g.   i.e.   viz.

4. Italic type is used to indicate words referred to as words, letters referred to as letters, or numerals referred to as numerals. However, if the word referred to as a word was actually spoken, it is often enclosed in quotation marks. If the letter is being used to refer to its sound and not its printed form, virgules or brackets can be used instead of italics. And if there is no chance of confusion, numerals referred to as numerals are often not italicized. (For an explanation of the ways in which to form the plurals of words, letters, and numerals referred

to as such, see the section on Plurals, beginning on page 140, in Chapter 3, "Plurals, Possessives, and Compounds."

> The panel could not decide whether *data* was a singular or plural noun.
>
> *Only* can be an adverb modifying a verb, as in the case of "I *only* tried to help."
>
> We heard his warning, but we weren't sure what "other repercussions" meant in that context.
>
> You should dot your *i*'s and cross your *t*'s.
>
> She couldn't pronounce her *s*'s.
>
> He was still having trouble with the /p/ sound.
>
> The first *2* and the last *1* are barely legible.

5. A letter used to indicate a shape is usually capitalized but not set in italics. For more on this use of capital letters, see the section on Other Uses of Capitals in this chapter.

6. Individual letters are sometimes set in italic type to provide additional typographical contrast. This use of italics is common when letters are used in run-in enumerations or when they are used to identify elements in an illustration.

> providing information about (*a*) typing, (*b*) transcribing, (*c*) formatting, and (*d*) graphics
>
> located at point *A* on the diagram

7. Italics are used to indicate a word created to suggest a sound.

From the nest came a high-pitched *whee* from one of the young birds.

We sat listening to the *chat-chat-chat* of the sonar.

8. Italics are used to emphasize or draw attention to a word or words in a sentence.

Students must notify the dean's office *in writing* of all courses added or dropped from their original list.

She had become *the* hero, the one everyone else looked up to.

NOTE: Italics serve to draw attention to words in large part because they are used so infrequently. Writers who overuse italics for giving emphasis may find that the italics lose their effectiveness.

Chapter 3

Plurals, Possessives, and Compounds

CONTENTS

This chapter describes the ways in which plurals, possessives, and compound words are most commonly formed. In doing so, it treats some of the simplest and some of the most problematic kinds of questions that are faced by writers and editors. For some of the questions raised in this chapter, various solutions have been developed over the years, but no single solution has come to be universally accepted. This chapter describes the range of solutions that are available; however, many of the questions raised in this chapter inevitably require arbitrary decisions and personal judgments. In cases like these, careful writers and editors usually make notes or keep a style sheet so that they can be consistent in the way that they form plurals, possessives, and compounds for certain specific words or categories of words.

Writers and editors are frequently told that consulting a good dictionary will solve many of the problems that are discussed in this chapter. To some extent this is true, and this chapter does recommend consulting a dictionary at a number of points. In this regard, the best dictionary to consult is an unabridged dictionary, such as *Webster's Third New International Dictionary*. In the absence of such a comprehensive reference book, writers and editors should consult a good desk dictionary, such as *Webster's Ninth New Collegiate Dictionary*. Any dictionary that is much smaller than the *Ninth Collegiate* will often be more frustrating in what it fails to show than helpful in what it shows.

In giving examples of plurals, possessives, and compounds, this chapter uses both *or* and *also* to separate variant forms of the same word. The word *or* is used when both forms of the word are used with approximately equal frequency in standard prose; the form that precedes the *or* is probably slightly more common than the form that follows it. The word *also* is used when one form of the word is much more common than the other; the more common precedes the less common.

Plurals

The plurals of most English words are formed by adding -*s* to the singular. If the noun ends in -*s*, -*x*, -*z*, -*ch*, or -*sh*, so that an extra syllable must be added in order to pronounce the plural, -*es* is added to the singular. If the noun ends in a *-y* preceded by a consonant, the *-y* is changed to *-i-* and *-es* is added. Most proper nouns ending in *-y* (as *Mary* or *January*), however, simply add *-s* to the singular.

Many English nouns do not follow the general pattern for forming plurals. Most good dictionaries give thorough coverage to irregular and variant plurals, so they are often the best place to start to answer questions about the plural form of a specific word. The paragraphs that follow describe the ways in which plurals are formed for a number of categories of words whose plural forms are most apt to raise questions.

The symbol → is used throughout this section of the chapter. In each case, the element that follows the arrow is the plural form of the element that precedes the arrow.

Abbreviations

1. The plurals of abbreviations are commonly formed by adding *-s* or an apostrophe plus *-s* to the abbreviation; however, there are some significant exceptions to this pattern. For more on the formation of plurals of abbreviations, see the section on Plurals, Possessives, and Compounds, beginning on page 192, in Chapter 4, "Abbreviations."

    COLA → COLA's
    CPU → CPUs
    bldg. → bldgs.
    f.o.b. → f.o.b.'s
    Ph.D. → Ph.D.'s
    p. → pp.

Animals

2. The names of many fishes, birds, and mammals
    have both a plural formed with a suffix and one
    that is identical with the singular. Some have only
    the -s plural; others have only an uninflected
    plural.

> flounder → flounder *or* flounders
> mink → mink *or* minks
> quail → quail *or* quails
> buffalo → buffalo *or* buffalos
> cow → cows
> hen → hens
> rat → rats
> monkey → monkeys
> bison → bison
> sheep → sheep
> shad → shad
> moose → moose

3. Many of the animals that have both plural forms
    are ones that are hunted, fished, or trapped, and
    those who hunt, fish for, and trap them are most
    likely to use the uninflected form. The -s form is
    especially likely to be used to emphasize diversity of
    kinds.

> caught four trout
>   *but*
> trouts of the Rocky Mountains
> a place where fish gather
>   *but*
> the fishes of the Pacific Ocean

Compounds and Phrases

4. Most compounds composed of two nouns, whether styled as one word or two words or as hyphenated words, are pluralized by pluralizing the final element.

> matchbox → matchboxes
> spokeswoman → spokeswomen
> judge advocate → judge advocates
> tree house → tree houses
> city-state → city-states
> crow's-foot → crow's-feet
> face-lift → face-lifts
> battle-ax → battle-axes

5. The plural form of a compound consisting of an-*er* agent noun and an adverb is made by pluralizing the noun element.

> hanger-on → hangers-on
> looker-on → lookers-on
> onlooker → onlookers
> passerby → passersby

6. Nouns made up of words that are not nouns form their plurals on the terminal element.

> also-ran → also-rans
> ne'er-do-well → ne'er-do-wells
> put-down → put-downs
> set-to → set-tos
> changeover → changeovers
> blowup → blowups

7. Plurals of compounds that are phrases consisting of two nouns separated by a preposition are regularly formed by pluralizing the first noun.

> aide-de-camp → aides-de-camp
> base on balls → bases on balls
> auto-da-fe → autos-da-fe
> mother-in-law → mothers-in-law
> man-of-war → men-of-war
> coup d'état → coups d'état
> attorney-at-law → attorneys-at-law
> lady-in-waiting → ladies-in-waiting
> power of attorney → powers of attorney

8. Compounds that are phrases consisting of two nouns separated by a preposition and a modifier form their plurals in various ways.

> flash in the pan → flashes in the pan
> jack-in-the-box → jack-in-the-boxes *or* jacks-in-the-box
> jack-of-all-trades → jacks-of-all-trades
> son of a gun → sons of guns
> stick-in-the-mud → stick-in-the-muds

9. Compounds consisting of a noun followed by an adjective are regularly pluralized by adding a suffix to the noun.

> cousin-german → cousins-german
> heir apparent → heirs apparent
> knight-errant → knights-errant

NOTE: If the adjective in such a compound tends to be construed as a noun, the compound may have more than one plural form.

attorney general → attorneys general *or* attorney
   generals
sergeant major → sergeants major *or* sergeant majors
poet laureate → poets laureate *or* poet laureates

Foreign Words and Phrases

10. Many nouns of foreign origin retain the foreign
    plural; most of them also have a regular English
    plural.

alumnus → alumni
beau → beaux *or* beaus
crisis → crises
emporium → emporiums *or* emporia
index → indexes *or* indices
larynx → larynges *or* larynxes
phenomenon → phenomena *or* phenomenons
schema → schemata *also* schemas
seraph → seraphim *or* seraphs
series → series
tempo → tempi *or* tempos

NOTE: A foreign plural may not be used for all
senses of a word or may be more commonly used
for some senses than for others.

antenna (on an insect) → antennae
antenna (on a radio) → antennas

11. Phrases of foreign origin may have a foreign plu-
    ral, an English plural, or both.

beau monde → beau mondes *or* beaux mondes
carte blanche → cartes blanches
charlotte russe → charlottes russe
felo-de-se → felones-de-se *or* felos-de-se
hors d'oeuvre → hors d'oeuvres

-ful Words

12. A plural *-fuls* can be used for any noun ending in *-ful*, but some of these nouns also have an alternative, usually less common plural with *-s-* preceding the suffix.

> eyeful → eyefuls
> mouthful → mouthfuls
> barnful → barnfuls
> worldful → worldfuls
> barrelful → barrelfuls *or* barrelsful
> bucketful → bucketfuls *or* bucketsful
> cupful → cupfuls *also* cupsful
> tablespoonful → tablespoonfuls *also* tablespoonsful

Irregular Plurals

13. A small group of English nouns form their plurals by changing one or more of their vowels.

> foot → feet
> man → men
> woman → women
> goose → geese
> mouse → mice
> tooth → teeth
> louse → lice

14. A few nouns have *-en* or *-ren* plurals.

> ox → oxen
> child → children
> brother → brethren

15. Some nouns ending in *-f*, *-fe*, and *-ff* have plurals that end in *-ves*. Some of these also have regularly formed plurals.

elf → elves
beef → beefs *or* beeves
knife → knives
staff → staffs *or* staves
life → lives
wharf → wharves *also* wharfs
loaf → loaves
dwarf → dwarfs *or* dwarves

Italic Elements

16. Italicized words, phrases, abbreviations, and letters
    in roman context are variously pluralized with ei-
    ther an italic or roman *s*. Most stylebooks urge use
    of a roman *s*, and our evidence indicates that that
    is the form used most commonly. If the plural is
    formed with an apostrophe and an -*s*, the -*s* is al-
    most always roman.

    > fifteen *Newsweek*s on the shelf
    > answered with a series of *uh-huh*s
    > a row of *x*'s

Letters

17. The plurals of letters are usually formed by the
    addition of an apostrophe and an -*s*, although up-
    percase letters are sometimes pluralized by the ad-
    dition of an -*s* alone.

    > p's and q's
    > V's of geese flying overhead
    > dot your *i*'s
    > straight As

Numbers

18. Numerals are pluralized by adding an *-s*, or, less commonly, an apostrophe and an *-s*.

> two par 5s
> 1960's
> 1970s
> the mid-$20,000s
> in the 80s
> DC-10's

19. Spelled-out numbers are usually pluralized without an apostrophe.

> in twos and threes
> scored two sixes

-o Words

20. Most words ending in an *-o* are pluralized by adding an *-s*; however, some words ending in an *-o* preceded by a consonant have *-s* plurals, some have *-es* plurals, and some have both. When you are in doubt about such a word, consult a dictionary.

> alto → altos
> echo → echoes
> motto → mottoes *also* mottos
> tornado → tornadoes *or* tornados

Proper Nouns

21. The plurals of proper nouns are usually formed with *-s* or *-es*.

> Bruce → Bruces
> Charles → Charleses

John Harris → John Harrises
Hastings → Hastingses
Velasquez → Velasquezes

22. Proper nouns ending in -*y* usually retain the -*y* and add -*s*.

February → Februarys
Mary → Marys
Mercury → Mercurys
  but
Ptolemy → Ptolemies
Sicily → The Two Sicilies
The Rockies

NOTE: Words that were originally proper nouns and that end in -*y* are usually pluralized by changing -*y* to -*i*- and adding -*es*, but a few retain the -*y*.

bobby → bobbies
johnny → johnnies
Jerry → Jerries
Tommy → Tommies
Bloody Mary → Bloody Marys
Typhoid Mary → Typhoid Marys

Quoted Elements

23. Style varies regarding the plural form of words in quotation marks. Some writers form the plural by adding an -*s* or an apostrophe plus -*s* within the quotation marks; others add an -*s* outside the quotation marks. Both arrangements look awkward, and writers generally try to avoid this construction.

too many "probably's" in the statement
didn't hear any "nays"

> One "you" among millions of "you"s
> a response characterized by its "yes, but"s

Symbols

24. Although symbols are not usually pluralized, when a symbol is being referred to as a character in itself without regard to meaning, the plural is formed by adding an *-s* or an apostrophe plus *-s*.

> used &'s instead of *and*'s
> his π's are hard to read
> printed three *s

Words used as Words

25. Words used as words without regard to meaning usually form their plurals by adding an apostrophe and an *-s*.

> five *and*'s in one sentence
> all those *wherefore*'s and *howsoever*'s

NOTE: When a word used as a word has become part of a fixed phrase, the plural is usually formed by adding a roman *-s* without the apostrophe.

> oohs and aahs
> dos and don'ts

Possessives

The possessive case of most nouns is formed by adding an apostrophe or an apostrophe plus *-s* to the end of the word. For most other uses of the apostrophe, such as to form contractions, see the section on Apostrophe, beginning on page 7, in Chapter 1, "Punctuation." For the use of the apostrophe to form plurals, see the section on Plurals in this chapter.

Common Nouns

1. The possessive case of singular and plural common nouns that do not end in an *s* or *z* sound is formed by adding an apostrophe plus *-s* to the end of the word.

> the boy's mother
> at her wit's end
> the potato's skin
> men's clothing
> children's books
> the symposia's themes

2. The possessive case of singular nouns ending in an *s* or *z* sound is usually formed by adding an apostrophe plus *-s* to the end of the word. Style varies somewhat on this point, as some writers prefer to add an apostrophe plus *-s* to the word only when the added *-s* is pronounced; if it isn't pronounced, they add just an apostrophe. According to our evidence, both approaches are common in contemporary prose, although always adding an apostrophe plus *-s* is the much more widely accepted approach.

> the press's books
> the index's arrangement
> the boss's desk
> the horse's saddle
> the audience's reaction *also* the audience' reaction
> the waitress's duties *also* the waitress' duties

the conference's outcome   *also*   the conference' outcome

NOTE: Even writers who follow the pattern of
adding an apostrophe plus -*s* to all singular nouns
will often make an exception for a multisyllabic
word that ends in an *s* or *z* sound if it is followed
by a word beginning with an *s* or *z* sound.

for convenience' sake
for conscience' sake
the illness' symptoms   *or*   the illness's symptoms
to the princess' surprise   *or*   to the princess's surprise

3. The possessive case of plural nouns ending in an *s*
or *z* sound is formed by adding only an apostrophe
to the end of the word. One exception to this rule
is that the possessive case of one-syllable irregular
plurals is usually formed by adding an apostrophe
plus -*s*.

horses' stalls
consumers' confidence
geese's calls
mice's habits

Proper Names

4. The possessive forms of proper names are generally made in the same way as they are for common
nouns. The possessive form of singular proper
names not ending in an *s* or *z* sound is made by
adding an apostrophe plus -*s* to the name. The possessive form of plural proper names is made by
adding just an apostrophe.

Mrs. Wilson's store
Utah's capital
Canada's rivers
the Wattses' daughter
the Cohens' house
Niagara Falls' location

5. As is the case for the possessive form of singular common nouns (see paragraph 2 above), the possessive form of singular proper names ending in an *s* or *z* sound may be formed either by adding an apostrophe plus *-s* or by adding just an apostrophe to the name. For the sake of consistency, most writers choose one pattern for forming the possessive of all singular names ending in an *s* or *z* sound, regardless of the pronunciation of individual names (for exceptions see paragraphs 6 and 7 below). According to our evidence, adding an apostrophe plus *-s* to all such names is more common than adding just the apostrophe.

Jones's car   *also*   Jones' car
Bliss's statue   *also*   Bliss' statue
Dickens's novels   *also*   Dickens' novels

6. The possessive form of classical and biblical names of two or more syllables ending in *-s* or *-es* is usually made by adding an apostrophe without an *-s*. If the name has only one syllable, the possessive form is made by adding an apostrophe and an *-s*.

Aristophanes' plays
Achilles' heel
Odysseus' journey

Judas' betrayal
Zeus's anger
Mars's help

7. The possessive forms of the names *Jesus* and *Moses* are always formed with just an apostrophe.

Jesus' time
Moses' law

8. The possessive forms of names ending in a silent -*s*, -*z*, or -*x* usually include the apostrophe and the -*s*.

Arkansas's capital
Camus's *The Stranger*
Delacroix's paintings
Josquin des Prez's work

9. For the sake of convenience and appearance, some writers will italicize the possessive ending when adding it to a name that is in italics; however, most frequently the possessive ending is in roman.

the U.S.S. *Constitution*'s cannons
the *Mona Lisa*'s somber hues
Gone With the Wind's ending
High Noon's plot

Pronouns

10. The possessive case of indefinite pronouns such as *anyone, everybody,* and *someone* is formed by adding an apostrophe and an -*s*.

everyone's
anybody's

everyone's
everybody's
someone's
somebody's

NOTE: Some indefinite pronouns usually require an *of* phrase rather than inflection to indicate possession.

the rights of each
the satisfaction of all
the inclination of many

11. Possessive pronouns include no apostrophes.

mine
yours
his
hers
its
ours
theirs

Phrases

12. The possessive form of a phrase is made by adding an apostrophe or an apostrophe plus -*s* to the last word in the phrase.

board of directors' meeting
his brother-in-law's sidecar
from the student of politics' point of view
a moment or so's thought

NOTE: Constructions such as these can become awkward, and it is often better to rephrase the sentence to eliminate the need for the possessive ending. For instance, the last two examples above could be rephrased as follows:

> from the point of view of the student of politics
> thinking for a moment or so

Words in Quotation Marks

13. Style varies regarding the possessive form of words in quotation marks. Some writers place the apostrophe and *-s* inside the quotation marks; others place them outside the quotation marks. Either arrangement will look awkward, and writers usually try to avoid this construction.

> the "Today Show"'s cohosts
> the "Grande Dame's" escort
> *but more commonly*
> the cohosts of the "Today Show"
> escort to the "Grande Dame"

Abbreviations

14. Possessives of abbreviations are formed in the same way as those of nouns that are spelled out. The singular possessive is formed by adding an apostrophe plus *-s* to the abbreviation; the plural possessive, by adding an apostrophe only.

> the AMA's executive committee
> Itek Corp.'s Applied Technology Division
> the Burns Bros.' stores
> the MPs' decisions

Numerals

15. The possessive form of nouns composed of or including numerals is made in the same way as for nouns composed wholly of words. The possessive of singular nouns is formed by adding an apostrophe plus -*s*; the possessive form of plural nouns, by adding an apostrophe only.

> 1985's most popular model
> Louis XIV's court
> the 1980s' most colorful figure

Individual and Joint Possession

16. Individual possession is indicated when an apostrophe plus -*s* is added to each noun in a sequence. Joint possession is most commonly indicated by adding an apostrophe or an apostrophe plus -*s* to the last noun in the sequence. In some cases, joint possession is also indicated by adding a possessive ending to each name.

> Kepler's and Clark's respective clients
> John's, Bill's, and Larry's boats
> Kepler and Clark's law firm
> Christine and James's vacation home   *or*   Christine's and James's vacation home

Compounds

A compound is a word or word group that consists of two or more parts working together as a unit to express a specific concept. Compounds can be formed by combining two or more words (as in *eye shadow, graphic equalizer, farmhouse, cost-effective, blue-pencil, around-the-*

clock, or *son of a gun*), by combining word elements (as prefixes or suffixes) with words (as in *ex-president, shoe-less, presorted, uninterruptedly,* or *meaningless*), or by combining two or more word elements (as in *supermicro* or *photomicrograph*). Compounds are written in one of three ways: solid (as *cottonmouth*), hyphenated (as *player-manager*), or open (as *field day*).

Some of the explanations in this section make reference to permanent and temporary compounds. Permanent compounds are those that are so commonly used that they have become established as permanent parts of the language; many of them can be found in dictionaries. Temporary compounds are those made up to fit the writer's need at the particular moment. Temporary compounds, of course, cannot be found in dictionaries and therefore present the writer with styling problems.

Presenting styling problems similar to those of temporary compounds are self-evident compounds. These are compounds (as *baseball game* or *economic policy*) that are readily understood from the meanings of the words that make them up. Self-evident compounds, like temporary compounds, are not to be found in dictionaries.

In other words, writers faced with having to use compounds such as *farm stand* (*farm-stand? farmstand?*), *wide body* (*wide-body? widebody?*), or *picture framing* (*picture-framing? pictureframing?*) cannot rely wholly on dictionaries to guide them in their styling of compounds. They need, in addition, to develop an approach for dealing with compounds that are not in the dictionary. A few of those approaches are explained below.

One approach is simply to leave open any compound that is not in the dictionary. Many writers do this, but there are drawbacks to this approach. A temporary compound may not be as easily recognized as a compound by the reader when it is left open. For instance if you need to use *wide body* as a term for a kind of jet airplane, a phrase like "the operation of wide bodies" may catch the reader unawares. And if you use the open style for a compound modifier, you may create momentary confusion (or even unintended amusement) with a phrase like "the operation of wide body jets."

Another possibility would be to hyphenate all compounds that aren't in the dictionary. Hyphenation would give your compound immediate recognition as a compound. But hyphenating all such compounds runs counter to some well-established American practice. Thus you would be calling too much attention to the compound and momentarily distracting the reader.

A third approach is to use analogy to pattern your temporary compound after some other similar compound. This approach is likely to be more complicated than simply picking an open or hyphenated form, and will not free you from the need to make your own decisions in most instances. But it does have the advantage of making your compound less distracting or confusing by making it look as much like other more familiar compounds as possible.

The rest of this section is aimed at helping you to use the analogical approach to styling compounds. You will find compounds listed according to the elements that make them up and the way that they function in a sentence.

This section deals first with compounds formed from whole English words, then compounds formed with word elements, and finally with a small collection of miscellaneous styling conventions relating to compounds. The symbol + in the following paragraphs can be interpreted as "followed immediately by."

Compound Nouns

Compound nouns are combinations of words that function in a sentence as nouns. They may consist of two or more nouns, a noun and a modifier, or two or more elements that are not nouns.

1. **noun + noun** Compounds composed of two nouns that are short, commonly used, and pronounced with falling stress—that is, with the most stress on the first noun and less or no stress on the second—are usually styled solid.

   > teapot
   > cottonmouth
   > birdbath
   > handmaiden
   > catfish
   > sweatband
   > handsaw
   > farmyard
   > football
   > handlebar
   > railroad
   > bandwagon

2. When a noun + noun compound is short and common but pronounced with equal stress on both nouns, the styling is more likely to be open.

bean sprouts
beach buggy
head louse
fuel oil
duffel bag
dart board
fuel cell
fire drill
rose fever

3. Many short noun + noun compounds begin as temporary compounds styled open. As they become more familiar and better established, there is a tendency for them to become solid.

data base   *is becoming*   database
chain saw   *is becoming*   chainsaw
lawn mower   *is becoming*   lawnmower

4. Noun + noun compounds that consist of longer nouns, are self-evident, or are temporary are usually styled open.

wildlife sanctuary
reunion committee
football game
television camera

5. When the nouns in a noun + noun compound describe a double title or double function, the compound is hyphenated.

city-state
dinner-dance
player-manager
decree-law

secretary-treasurer
author-critic

6. Compounds formed from a noun or adjective followed by *man, woman, person,* or *people* and denoting an occupation are regularly solid.

salesman
saleswoman
salesperson
salespeople
congresswoman
handyman
spokesperson
policewoman

7. Compounds that are units of measurement are hyphenated.

foot-pound
man-hour
light-year
kilowatt-hour
column-inch
board-foot

8. **adjective + noun**   Most temporary or self-evident adjective + noun compounds are styled open. Permanent compounds formed from relatively long adjectives or nouns are also open.

automatic weapons
modal auxiliary
modular arithmetic
religious freedom
automatic pilot

graphic equalizer
pancreatic juice
minor seminary
white lightning

9. Adjective + noun compounds consisting of two
   short words may be styled solid when pronounced
   with falling stress. Just as often, however, short adjective + noun compounds are styled open; a few
   are hyphenated.

bigfoot
blueprint
drywall
highland
longboat
longhand
redline
shortcake
shortcut
shorthand
sickbed
wetland
yellowhammer
big deal
dry cleaner
dry rot
dry run
dry well
high gear
long haul
red tape
short run
short story
sick leave
wet nurse

yellow jacket
red-eye
red-hot

10. **participle + noun** Most participle + noun compounds are styled open, whether permanent, temporary, or self-evident.

frying pan
furnished apartment
shredded wheat
whipped cream
nagging backache
whipping boy

11. **noun's + noun** Compounds consisting of a possessive noun followed by another noun are usually styled hyphenated or open.

crow's-feet
lion's share
fool's gold
cat's cradle
cat's-eye
cat's-paw
stirred up a hornet's nest

NOTE: Compounds of this type that have become solid have lost the apostrophe.

foolscap
menswear
sheepshead

12. **noun + verb + -er; noun + verb + -ing** Temporary compounds in which the first noun is the object of the verb to which the suffix has been

added are most often styled open; however, many writers use a hyphen to make the relationships of the words immediately apparent. Permanent compounds like these are sometimes styled solid as well.

> *temporary*
> fact checker
> risk-taking
> opinion maker
> career planning
> cost-cutting
> English-speakers
> *permanent*
> lifesaver
> data processing
> lawn mower
> copyediting
> bird-watcher
> penny-pinching
> flyswatter
> fund-raising
> bookkeeper

13. **object + verb** Noun compounds consisting of a verb preceded by a noun that is its object are variously styled.

> clambake
> car wash
> face-lift
> turkey shoot

14. **verb + object** A few compounds are formed from a verb followed by a noun that is its object. These are mostly older words, and they are solid.

tosspot
breakwater
pinchpenny
cutthroat
carryall
pickpocket

15. **noun + adjective** Compounds composed of a
noun followed by an adjective are styled open or
hyphenated.

battle royal
consul general
secretary-general
governor-designate
heir apparent
letters patent
sum total
mayor-elect
president-elect

16. **particle + noun** Compounds consisting of a particle (usually a preposition or adverb having prepositional, adverbial, or adjectival force in the compound) and a noun are usually styled solid,
especially when they are short and pronounced
with falling stress.

downpour
inpatient
outpatient
input
output
throughput
aftershock

overskirt
offshoot
undershirt
crossbones
upkeep

17. A few particle + noun compounds, especially when composed of longer elements or having equal stress on both elements, may be hyphenated or open.

off-season
down payment
off year
cross-fertilization

18. **verb + particle; verb + adverb** These compounds may be hyphenated or solid. Compounds with two-letter particles (*by, to, in, up, on*) are most frequently hyphenated, since the hyphen aids quick comprehension. Compounds with three-letter particles (*off, out*) are hyphenated or solid with about equal frequency. Those with longer particles or adverbs are more often but not always solid.

call-up
lay-up
lead-in
run-on
set-to
sign-on
sit-in
trade-in
turn-on

warm-up
wrap-up
write-in
flyby
letup
pileup
brush-off
shoot-out
show-off
sick-out
write-off
dropout
layout
strikeout
tryout
turnoff
follow-through
get-together
breakdown
breakthrough
gadabout
giveaway
rollback
takeover

19. **verb + -er + particle; verb + -ing + particle**   Except for *passerby*, these compounds are hyphenated.

hanger-on
diner-out
falling-out
runner-up
summing-up
talking-to
goings-on
looker-on

20. compounds of three or four elements Compounds of three or four elements are styled either hyphenated or open. Those consisting of noun + prepositional phrase are generally open, although some are hyphenated. Those formed from other combinations are usually hyphenated.

> base on balls
> justice of the peace
> lady of the house
> lily of the valley
> lord of misrule
> son of a gun
> good-for-nothing
> jack-of-all-trades
> lady-in-waiting
> love-in-a-mist
> by-your-leave
> Johnny-jump-up
> know-it-all
> pick-me-up
> stick-to-itiveness

21. letter + noun Compounds formed from a single letter (or sometimes a combination of them) followed by a noun are either open or hyphenated.

> A-frame
> B-girl
> H-bomb
> T-shirt
> C ration
> D day
> I beam
> T square
> ABO system

J-bar lift
Rh factor
H and L hinge

Compounds That Function as Adjectives

Compound adjectives are combinations of words that
work together to modify a noun—that is, they work as
unit modifiers. As unit modifiers they should be distinguished from other strings of adjectives that may also
precede a noun. For instance, in "a low, level tract of
land" or "that long, lonesome road" the two adjectives
each modify the noun separately. We are talking about
a tract of land that is both low and level and about a
road that is both long and lonesome. These are coordinate modifiers.

In "a low monthly fee" or "a wrinkled red necktie"
the first adjective modifies the noun plus the second adjective. In other words, we mean a monthly fee that is
low and a red necktie that is wrinkled. These are non-
coordinate modifiers. But in "low-level radiation" we do
not mean radiation that is low and level or level radiation that is low; we mean radiation that is at a low level.
Both words work as a unit to modify the noun.

Unit modifiers are usually hyphenated. The hyphens not only make it easier for the reader to grasp
the relationship of the words but also avoid confusion.
The hyphen in "a call for more-specialized controls" re-
moves any ambiguity as to which word *more* modifies. A
phrase like "graphic arts exhibition" may seem clear to
its author, but may have an unintended meaning for
some readers.

22. **Before the Noun (attributive position)** Most two-word permanent or temporary compound adjectives are hyphenated when placed before the noun.

> tree-lined streets
> fast-acting medication
> an iron-clad guarantee
> a tough-minded negotiator
> class-conscious persons
> Spanish-American relations
> well-intended advice
> the red-carpet treatment
> a profit-loss statement
> an input-output device
> arrested on a trumped-up charge
> a risk-free investment

23. Temporary compounds formed of an adverb (as *well, more, less, still*) followed by a participle (or sometimes an adjective) are usually hyphenated when placed before a noun.

> more-specialized controls
> a just-completed survey
> a still-growing company
> a well-funded project
> these fast-moving times
> a now-vulnerable politician

24. Temporary compounds formed from an adverb ending in *-ly* followed by a participle may sometimes be hyphenated but are more commonly open, because adverb + adjective + noun is a normal word order.

a widely-read feature
internationally-known authors
   but more often
generally recognized categories
a beautifully illustrated book
publicly supported universities
our rapidly changing plans

25. The combination of *very* + adjective is not a unit modifier.

a very satisfied smile

26. Many temporary compound adjectives are formed by using a compound noun—either permanent or temporary—to modify another noun. If the compound noun is an open compound, it is usually hyphenated so that the relationship of the words is more immediately apparent to the reader.

the farm-bloc vote
a picture-framing shop
a short-run printing press
a secret-compartment ring
a tax-law case
ocean-floor hydrophones

27. Some open compound nouns are considered so readily recognizable that they are frequently placed before a noun without a hyphen.

a high school diploma   *or*   a high-school diploma
a data processing course   *or*   a data-processing course
a dry goods store   *or*   a dry-goods store

28. A proper name placed before a noun to modify it is not hyphenated.

> a Thames River marina
> a Huck Finn life
> a Korean War veteran
> a General Motors car

29. Compound adjectives of three or more words are hyphenated when they precede the noun. Many temporary compounds are formed by taking a phrase, hyphenating it, and placing it before a noun.

> spur-of-the-moment decisions
> higher-than-anticipated costs
> her soon-to-be-released movie

30. Compound adjectives composed of foreign words are not hyphenated when placed before a noun unless they are always hyphenated.

> the per capita cost
> an a priori argument
> a cordon bleu restaurant
> a ci-devant professor

31. Chemical names used as modifiers before a noun are not hyphenated.

> a sodium hypochlorite bleach
> a citric acid solution

32. Following the Noun (as a complement or predicate adjective) When the words that make up a compound adjective follow the noun they modify, they tend to fall in normal word order and are no longer unit modifiers. They are therefore no longer hyphenated.

> Controls have become more specialized.
> The company is still growing.
> a device for both input and output
> a statement of profit and loss
> arrested on charges that had been trumped up
> decisions made on the spur of the moment
> They were ill prepared for the journey.

33. Many permanent and temporary compounds keep their hyphens after the noun in a sentence if they continue to function as unit modifiers. Compounds consisting of adjective or noun + participle, adjective or noun + noun + *-ed* (which looks like a participle), or noun + adjective are most likely to remain hyphenated.

> Your ideas are high-minded but impractical.
> streets that are tree-lined
> You were just as nice-looking then.
> metals that are corrosion-resistant
> tends to be accident-prone

34. Permanent compound adjectives that are entered in dictionaries are usually styled in the way that they appear in the dictionary whether they precede or follow the noun they modify.

> The group was public-spirited.
> The problems are mind-boggling.
> is well-read in economics

35. Compound adjectives of three or more words are normally not hyphenated when they follow the noun they modify.

> These remarks are off the record.

36. Permanent compounds of three or more words may be entered as hyphenated adjectives in dictionaries. In such cases the hyphens are retained as long as the phrase is being used as a unit modifier.

> the plan is still pay-as-you-go
> *but* a plan in which you pay as you go

37. It is possible that a permanent hyphenated adjective from the dictionary may appear alongside a temporary compound in a position where it would normally be open (as "one who is both ill-humored and ill prepared"). Editors usually try to resolve these inconsistencies, either by hyphenating both compounds or leaving both compounds open.

38. When an adverb modifies another adverb that is the first element of a compound modifier, the compound may lose its hyphen. If the first adverb modifies the whole compound, however, the hyphen should be retained.

> a very well developed idea
> a delightfully well-written book
> a most ill-humored remark

39. Adjective compounds that are names of colors may be styled open or hyphenated. Color names in which each element can function as a noun (as *blue* *green* or *chrome yellow*) are almost always hyphenated when they precede a noun; they are sometimes open when they follow the noun. Color names in which the first element can only be an adjective are less consistently treated; they are often not hyphenated before a noun and are usually not hyphenated after.

> blue-gray paint
> paint that is blue-gray   *also*   paint that is blue gray
> bluish gray paint   *or*   bluish-gray paint
> paint that is bluish gray

40. Compound modifiers that include a number followed by a noun are hyphenated when they precede the noun they modify. When the modifier follows the noun, it is usually not hyphenated. For more on the styling of numbers, see Chapter 5, "The Treatment of Numbers."

> five-card stud
> ten-foot pole
> twelve-year-old girl
> an 18-inch rule
>   *but*
> a 10 percent raise
> an essay that is one page
> a child who is ten years old

41. An adjective that is composed of a number followed by a noun in the possessive is not hyphenated.

> a two weeks' wait
> a four blocks' walk

Compounds That Function as Adverbs

42. Adverb compounds consisting of preposition + noun are almost always written solid; however, there are a few well-known exceptions.

> downtown
> downwind
> onstage
> overseas
> upstairs
> upfield
> offhand
> underhand
> *but*
> in-house
> off-line
> on-line

43. Compound adverbs of more than two words are usually styled open, and they usually follow the words they modify.

> every which way
> high and dry
> off and on
> little by little
> hook, line, and sinker
> over and over

44. A few three-word adverbs are homographs of hyphenated adjectives and are therefore styled with hyphens. But many adverbs are styled open even if an adjective formed from the same phrase is hyphenated.

    back-to-back (adverb or adjective)
    face-to-face (adverb or adjective)
      but
    hand-to-hand combat
    fought hand to hand
    off-the-cuff remarks
    spoke off the cuff

Compound Verbs

45. Two-word verbs consisting of a verb followed by an adverb or a preposition are styled open.

    get together
    run around
    run across
    set to
    run wild
    put down
    break through
    strike out
    print out

46. A compound composed of a particle followed by a verb is styled solid.

    upgrade
    outflank
    overcome
    bypass

47. A verb derived from an open or hyphenated compound noun—permanent, temporary, or self-evident—is hyphenated.

    blue-pencil
    double-check

    poor-mouth
    sweet-talk
    tap-dance
    water-ski

48. A verb derived from a solid noun is styled solid.

    bankroll
    roughhouse
    mainstream

Compounds Formed with Word Elements

Many new and temporary compounds are formed by adding word elements to existing words or by combining word elements. There are three basic word elements: prefixes (as *anti-*, *re-*, *non-*, *super-*), suffixes (as *-er*, *-ly*, *-ness*, *-ism*), and what the dictionaries call combining forms (as *mini-*, *macro-*, *pseud-*, *ortho-*, *-ped*, *-graphy*, *-gamic*, *-plasty*). Prefixes and suffixes are usually attached to existing words; combining forms are usually combined to form new words.

49. prefix + word Except as specified below, compounds formed from a prefix and a word are usually styled solid.

    precondition
    refurnish
    suborder
    postwar
    interagency
    misshapen
    overfond
    unhelpful

50. If the prefix ends with a vowel and the word it is attached to begins with the same vowel, the compound is usually hyphenated.

> anti-inflation
> co-owner
> de-emphasize
> multi-institutional

NOTE: Many exceptions to this styling (as *cooperate* and *reentry*) can be found by checking a dictionary.

51. If the base word to which a prefix is added is capitalized, the compound is hyphenated.

> anti-American
> post-Victorian
> pro-Soviet
> inter-Caribbean

NOTE: The prefix is usually not capitalized in such compounds. But if the prefix and the base word together form a new proper name, the compound may be solid with the prefix capitalized (as *Postimpressionist, Precambrian*). Such exceptions can be found in a dictionary.

52. Compounds made with *self-* and *ex-* meaning "former" are hyphenated.

> self-pity
> ex-wife

53. If a prefix is added to a hyphenated compound, it may be either followed by a hyphen or closed up solid to the next element. Permanent compounds of this kind should be checked in a dictionary.

> unair-conditioned
> non-self-governing
> ultra-up-to-date
> unself-conscious

54. If a prefix is added to an open compound, the prefix is followed by a hyphen in typewritten material. In typeset material, this hyphen is often represented by an en dash. (For more on this use of the en dash, see paragraph 16 in the section on Dash, beginning on page 42, in Chapter 1, "Punctuation.")

> ex–Boy Scout
> post–coup d'état

55. A compound that would be identical with another word if styled solid is usually hyphenated to prevent misreading.

> a multi-ply fabric
> re-collect the money
> un-ionized particles

56. Some writers and editors like to hyphenate a compound that might otherwise be solid if they think the reader might be momentarily puzzled (as by consecutive vowels, doubled consonants, or simply an odd combination of letters.)

> coed *or* co-ed
> overreact *or* over-react
> coworker *or* co-worker
> interrow *or* inter-row

57. Temporary compounds formed from *vice-* are usually hyphenated; however, some permanent compounds (as *vice president* and *vice admiral*) are open.

58. When prefixes are attached to numerals, the compounds are hyphenated.

> pre-1982 expenses
> post-1975 vintages
> non-20th-century ideas

59. Compounds formed from combining forms like *Anglo-*, *Judeo-*, or *Sino-* are hyphenated when the second element is an independent word and solid when it is a combining form.

> Judeo-Christian
> Austro-Hungarian
> Sino-Soviet
> Italophile
> Francophone
> Anglophobe

60. Prefixes that are repeated in the same compound are separated by a hyphen.

> sub-subheading

61. Some prefixes and initial combining forms have related independent adjectives or adverbs that may be used where the prefix might be expected. A temporary compound with *quasi(-)* or *pseudo(-)* therefore may be written open as modifier + noun or hyphenated as combining form + noun. A writer or editor must thus decide which style to follow.

quasi intellectual *or* quasi-intellectual
pseudo liberal *or* pseudo-liberal

NOTE: in some cases (as *super*, *super-*), the independent modifier may not mean quite the same as the prefix.

62. Compounds consisting of different prefixes with the same base word and joined by *and* or *or* are sometimes shortened by pruning the first compound back to the prefix. The missing base word is indicated by a hyphen on the prefix.

pre- and postoperative care
anti- or pro-Revolutionary sympathies

63. **word + suffix** Except as noted below, compounds formed by adding a suffix to a word are styled solid.

Darwinist
fortyish
landscaper
powerlessness

64. Permanent or temporary compounds formed with a suffix are hyphenated if the addition of the suffix would create a sequence of three like letters.

bell-like
will-less
a coffee-er coffee

65. Temporary compounds made with a suffix are often hyphenated if the base word is more than three syllables long, if the base word ends with the same

letter the suffix begins with, or if the suffix creates a confusing sequence of letters.

> tunnel-like
> Mexican-ness
> jaw-wards
> umbrella-like
> industry-wide
> battle-worthy

66. Compounds made from a number + *odd* are hyphenated whether the number is spelled out or in numerals; a number + *-fold* is solid if the number is spelled out but hyphenated if it is in numerals.

> 20-odd
> twenty-odd
> 12-fold
> twelvefold

67. Most compounds formed from an open or hyphenated compound + a suffix do not separate the suffix by a hyphen. But such suffixes as *-like*, *-wide*, *-worthy*, and *-proof*, all of which are homographs of independent adjectives, are attached by a hyphen.

> good-humoredness
> dollar-a-yearism
> do-it-yourselfer
> a United Nations-like agency

NOTE: Open compounds often become hyphenated when a suffix is added unless they are proper nouns.

> middle age   *but*   middle-ager
> New Englandism
> tough guy   *but*   tough-guyese
> Wall Streeter

68. combining form + combining form Many new terms in technical fields are created by adding combining form to combining form or combining form to a word or a word part. Such compounds are generally intended to be permanent, even though many never get into the dictionary. They are regularly styled solid.

Miscellaneous Styling Conventions

69. Compounds that would otherwise be styled solid according to the principles described above are written open or hyphenated to avoid ambiguity, to make sure of rapid comprehension, or to make the pronunciation more obvious.

> meat-ax *or* meat ax
> bi-level
> tri-city
> re-utter
> umbrella-like
> un-iced

70. When typographical features such as capitals or italics make word relationships in a sentence clear, it is not necessary to hyphenate an open compound (as when it precedes a noun it modifies).

> a *Chicago Tribune* story
> an "eyes only" memo
> I've been Super Bowled to death.
> a *noblesse oblige* attitude

71. Publications (as technical journals) aimed at a specialized readership likely to recognize the elements of a compound and their relationship tend to use open and solid stylings more frequently than more general publications would.

electrooculogram
radiofrequency
rapid eye movement

72. Words that are formed by reduplication and so consist of two similar-sounding elements (as *hush-hush*, *razzle-dazzle*, or *hugger-mugger*) present styling questions like those of compounds. Words like these are hyphenated if each of the elements is made up of more than one syllable. If each element has only one syllable, the words are variously styled solid or hyphenated. The solid styling is slightly more common overall; however, for very short words (as *no-no*, *go-go*, and *so-so*), for words in which both elements may have primary stress (as *tip-top* and *sci-fi*), and for words coined in the twentieth century (as *ack-ack* and *hush-hush*), the hyphenated styling is more common.

goody-goody
palsy-walsy
teeter-totter
topsy-turvy
agar-agar
ack-ack
boo-boo
tip-top
crisscross
peewee
knickknack
singsong

Chapter 4

Abbreviations

CONTENTS

Abbreviations are used for a variety of reasons. They serve to save space, to avoid repetition of long words and phrases that may distract the reader, and to reduce keystrokes for typists and thereby increase their output. In addition, abbreviations are used simply to conform to conventional usage.

The frequency of abbreviations in typewritten or printed material is directly related to the nature of the material itself. For example, technical literature (as in the military and in the fields of aerospace, engineering, data processing, and medicine) features many abbreviations, but formal literary writing has relatively few. By the same token, the number of abbreviations in a piece of business writing depends on the nature of the business, as do the particular abbreviations employed. A person working in a university English department will often see *ibid., ll.,* and *TESOL,* while the employee of an electronics firm will instead see *CAD, CPU,* and *mm* from day to day.

Unfortunately, the contemporary styling of abbreviations is to a large extent inconsistent and arbitrary. No set of rules can hope to cover all the possible variations, exceptions, and peculiarities actually encountered in print. The styling of abbreviations—whether capitalized or lowercased, closed up or spaced, punctuated or unpunctuated—depends most often on the writer's preference or the organization's policy. For example, some companies style the abbreviation for *cash on delivery* as *COD,* while others prefer *C.O.D.,* and still others, *c.o.d.*

All is not confusion, however, and general patterns can be discerned. Some abbreviations (as *a.k.a., e.g., etc., i.e., No.,* and *viz.*) are governed by a strong tradition of punctuation, while others (as *NATO, NASA, NOW, OPEC,* and *SALT*) that are pronounced as words tend to be all-capitalized and unpunctuated. Styling problems can be dealt with by consulting a good general dictionary such as *Webster's Ninth New Collegiate Dictionary,* especially for capitalization guidance, and by following the guidelines of one's own organization or the dictates of one's own preference. An abbreviations dictionary such as *Webster's Guide to Abbreviations* may also be consulted.

Punctuation

The paragraphs that follow describe a few broad principles that apply to abbreviations in general; however, there are many specific situations in which these principles will not apply. For instance, U.S. Postal Service abbreviations for names of states are always unpunctuated, as are the abbreviations used within most branches of the armed forces for the names of ranks. The section on Specific Styling Conventions in this chapter contains more information on particular kinds of abbreviations.

1. A period follows most abbreviations that are formed by omitting all but the first few letters of a word.

> bull. for *bulletin*
> fig. for *figure*
> bro. for *brother*
> Fr. for *French*

2. A period follows most abbreviations that are formed by omitting letters from the middle of a word.

> secy. for *secretary*
> agcy. for *agency*
> mfg. for *manufacturing*
> Mr. for *Mister*

3. Punctuation is usually omitted from abbreviations that are made up of initial letters of words that constitute a phrase or compound word. However, for some of these abbreviations, especially ones that are not capitalized, the punctuation is retained.

GNP for *gross national product*
PC for *personal computer*
EFT for *electronic funds transfer*
f.o.b. for *free on board*

4. Terms in which a suffix is added to a numeral, such as *1st, 2nd, 3d, 8vo,* and *12mo,* are not abbreviations and do not require a period.

5. Isolated letters of the alphabet used to designate a shape or position in a sequence are not punctuated.

T square
A 1
I beam
V sign

6. Some abbreviations are punctuated with one or more virgules in place of periods.

c/o for *care of*
w/o for *without*
d/b/a for *doing business as*
w/w for *wall to wall*

Capitalization

1. Abbreviations are capitalized if the words they represent are proper nouns or adjectives.

F for *Fahrenheit*
Nov. for *November*
NFL for *National Football League*
Brit. for *British*

2. Abbreviations are usually capitalized when formed from the initial letters of the words or word elements that make up what is being abbreviated. There are, however, some very common abbreviations formed in this way that are not capitalized.

TM for *trademark*
EEG for *electroencephalogram*
ETA for *estimated time of arrival*
FY for *fiscal year*
CATV for *community antenna television*
a.k.a. for *also known as*
d/b/a for *doing business as*

3. Most abbreviations that are pronounced as words, rather than as a series of letters, are capitalized. If they have been assimilated into the language as words in their own right, however, they are most often lowercased.

OPEC
NATO
MIRV
NOW account
quasar
laser
sonar
scuba

Plurals, Possessives, and Compounds

1. Punctuated abbreviations of single words are pluralized by adding -*s* before the period.

   > bldgs.
   > bros.
   > figs.
   > mts.

2. Punctuated abbreviations that stand for phrases or compounds are pluralized by adding -*'s* after the last period.

   > Ph.D.'s
   > f.o.b.'s
   > J.P.'s
   > M.B.A.'s

3. Unpunctuated abbreviations that stand for phrases or compound words are usually pluralized by adding -*s* to the end of the abbreviation.

   > COLAs
   > CPUs
   > PCs
   > DOSs

   NOTE: Some writers pluralize such abbreviations by adding -*'s* to the abbreviation; however, this styling is far less common than the one described above.

4. The plural form of most lowercase single-letter abbreviations is made by repeating the letter. For the

plural form of single-letter abbreviations that are abbreviations for units of measure, see paragraph 5 below.

cc. for *copies*
ff. for *and the following ones*
ll. for *lines*
nn. for *notes*
pp. for *pages*
vv. for *verses*

5. The plural form of abbreviations of units of measure is the same as the singular form.

30 sec.
24 ml
20 min.
200 bbl.
30 d.
24 h.
50 m
10 mi.

6. Possessives of abbreviations are formed in the same way as those of spelled-out nouns: the singular possessive is formed by the addition of -*'s*, the plural possessive simply by the addition of an apostrophe.

the CPU's memory
most CPUs' memories
Brody Corp.'s earnings
Bay Bros.' annual sale

7. Compounds that consist of an abbreviation added to another word are formed in the same way as compounds that consist of spelled-out nouns.

a Kalamazoo, Mich.-based company
an AMA-approved medical school

8. Compounds formed by adding a prefix or suffix to an abbreviation are usually styled with a hyphen.

an IBM-like organization
non-DNA molecules
pre-HEW years

Specific Styling Conventions

The following paragraphs describe styling practices commonly followed for specific kinds of situations involving abbreviations. The paragraphs are arranged under the following alphabetical headings.

Latitude and Longitude
Laws and Bylaws
Military Ranks and Units
Number
Personal Names
Saint
Scientific Terms
Time
Titles
Units of Measure
Versus

A and An

1. The choice of the article *a* or *an* before abbreviations depends on the *sound* with which the abbreviation begins. If an abbreviation begins with a consonant sound, *a* is normally used. If an abbreviation begins with a vowel sound, *an* is used.

   a B.A. degree
   a YMCA club
   a UN agency
   an FCC report
   an SAT score
   an IRS agent

A.D. and B.C.

2. The abbreviations A.D. and B.C. are usually styled in typeset matter as punctuated, unspaced small capitals; in typed material they usually appear as punctuated, unspaced capitals.

   in printed material
   41 B.C.
   A.D. 185

in typed material
41 B.C.
A.D. 185

3. The abbreviation A.D. usually precedes the date; the abbreviation B.C. usually follows the date. However, many writers and editors place A.D. after the date, thus making their placement of A.D. consistent with their placement of B.C. In references to whole centuries, the usual practice is to place A.D. after the century. The only alternative is not to use the abbreviation at all in such references.

A.D. 185   *but also*   185 A.D.
the fourth century A.D.

Agencies, Associations, and Organizations

4. The names of agencies, associations, and organizations are usually abbreviated after they have been spelled out on their first occurrence in a text. The abbreviations are usually all capitalized and unpunctuated.

EPA
SEC
NAACP
NCAA
USO
NOW

NOTE: In contexts where the abbreviation is expected to be instantly recognizable, it will generally be used without having its full form spelled out on its first occurrence.

Beginning a Sentence

5. Most writers and editors avoid beginning a sentence with an abbreviation that is ordinarily not capitalized. Abbreviations that are ordinarily capitalized, on the other hand, are commonly used to begin sentences.

> Page 22 contains... *not* P. 22 contains...
> Doctor Smith believes... *or* Dr. Smith believes...
> OSHA regulations require...
> PCB concentrations that were measured at...

Books of the Bible

6. Books of the Bible are generally spelled out in running text but abbreviated in references to chapter and verse.

> The minister based his sermon on Genesis.
> In the beginning God created the heavens and the earth. —Gen. 1:1

Capitalization—See section on Capitalization in this chapter.

Chemical Elements and Compounds—See Scientific Terms below.

Company Names

7. The styling of company names varies widely. Many published style manuals say that the name of a company should not be abbreviated unless the abbreviation is part of its official name; however,

many publications routinely abbreviate words such as *Corporation, Company,* and *Incorporated* when they appear in company names. Words such as *Airlines, Associates, Fabricators, Manufacturing,* and *Railroad,* however, are spelled out.

> Ginn and Company *or* Ginn and Co.
> The Bailey Banks and Biddle Company *or* The Bailey Banks and Biddle Co.
> Cross & Trecker Corp.
> Canon, U.S.A., Inc.

NOTE: An ampersand frequently replaces the word *and* in official company names. For more on this use of the ampersand, see paragraph 1 in the section on Ampersand, beginning on page 5, in Chapter 1, "Punctuation."

8. If a company is easily recognizable from its initials, its name is usually spelled out for the first mention and abbreviated in all subsequent references. Some companies have made their initials part of their official name, and in those cases the initials appear in all references.

> *first reference*   General Motors Corp. released figures today . . .
> *subsequent reference* A GM spokesperson said . . .
> MCM Electronics, an Ohio-based electronics company . . .

Compass Points

9. Compass points are abbreviated when occurring after street names, though styling varies regarding whether these abbreviations are punctuated and whether they are preceded by a comma. When compass points form essential internal elements of street names, they are usually spelled out in full.

> 2122 Fourteenth Street, NW *or* 2122 Fourteenth Street NW *or* 2122 Fourteenth Street, N.W.
> 192 East 49th Street
> 1282 North Avenue

Compounds—See section on Plurals, Possessives, and Compounds above.

Computer Terms—See **Scientific Terms** below.

Contractions

10. Some abbreviations resemble contractions by including an apostrophe in place of omitted letters. These abbreviations are not punctuated with a period.

> sec'y for *secretary*
> ass'n for *association*
> dep't for *department*

NOTE: This style of abbreviation is usually avoided in formal writing.

Courtesy Titles—See **Titles** below.

Dates

11. The names of days and months are usually not abbreviated in running text, although some publications do abbreviate names of months when they appear in dates that refer to a specific day or days.

The names of months are not abbreviated in date lines of business letters, but they may be abbreviated in government or military correspondence.

> the December issue of *Scientific American*
> going to camp in August
> a report due on Tuesday
> a meeting held on August 1, 1985 *or* a meeting held on Aug. 1, 1985
>
> *general business date line*   November 1, 1985
> *military date line*   1 Nov 1985

NOTE: When dates are used in tables or in notes, the names of days and months are commonly abbreviated.

Degrees

12. Except for a few academic degrees with highly recognizable abbreviations (as *A.B.*, *M.S.*, and *Ph.D.*), the names of degrees and professional ratings are spelled out in full when first mentioned in running text. Often the name of the degree is followed by its abbreviation enclosed in parentheses, so that the abbreviation may be used alone later in running text. When a degree or professional rating follows a person's name it is usually abbreviated.

> Special attention is devoted to the master of arts in teaching (M.A.T.) degree.
> Julia Ramirez, P.E.

13. Like other abbreviations, abbreviations of degrees and professional ratings are often unpunctuated. In general, punctuated abbreviations are more common for academic degrees, and unpunctuated

abbreviations are slightly more common for professional ratings, especially if the latter comprise three or more capitalized letters.

> R.Ph.
> P.E.
> CLA
> CMET
> Ph.D.
> B.Sc.
> M.B.A.
> BGS

14. The first letter of each element in abbreviations of degrees and professional ratings is capitalized. Other letters are usually not capitalized.

> D.Ch.E.
> Litt.D.
> M.F.A.
> D.Th.

Division of Abbreviations

15. Division of abbreviations at the end of lines or between pages is usually avoided.

> received an M.B.A.   *not*   received an M.B.-
> degree   A. degree

Expansions—See **Full Forms** below.

Footnotes

16. Footnotes sometimes incorporate abbreviations.

> ibid.
> op. cit.

NOTE: In current practice these abbreviations are usually not italicized.

Full Forms

17. When using an abbreviation that may be unfamiliar or confusing to the reader, many publications give the full form first, followed by the abbreviation in parentheses; in subsequent references just the abbreviation is used.

> *first reference*   At the American Bar Association (ABA) meeting in June . . .
> *subsequent reference*   At that particular ABA meeting . . .

Geographical and Topographical Names

18. U.S. Postal Service abbreviations for states, possessions, and Canadian provinces are all-capitalized and unpunctuated, as are Postal Service abbreviations for streets and other geographical features when these abbreviations are used on envelopes addressed for automated mass handling.

> *addressed for automated handling*
> 1234 SMITH BLVD
> SMITHVILLE, MN 56789
> *regular address styling*
> 1234 Smith Blvd.
> Smithville, MN 56789

19. Abbreviations of states are often used in running text to identify the location of a city or county. In this context they are set off with commas, and punctuated, upper- and lowercase state abbreviations are usually used. In other situations within running text, the names of states are usually not abbreviated.

> John Smith of 15 Chestnut St., Sarasota, Fla., has won . . .
> the Louisville, Ky., public library system
> Boston, the largest city in Massachusetts, . . .

20. Terms such as *street* and *parkway* are variously abbreviated or unabbreviated in running text. When they are abbreviated, they are usually punctuated.

> our office at 1234 Smith Blvd. (*or* Boulevard)
> an accident on Windward Road (*or* Rd.)

21. Names of countries are typically abbreviated in tabular data, but they are usually spelled in full in running text. The most common exceptions to this pattern are the abbreviations *U.S.S.R.* and *U.S.* (see paragraph 23 below).

> *in a table*
> Gt. Brit. *or* U.K. *or* UK
> *in text*
> Great Britain and the U.S.S.R. announced the agreement.

22. Abbreviations for the names of most countries are punctuated. Abbreviations for countries whose names include more than one word are often not punctuated if the abbreviations are formed from only the initial letters of the individual words.

> Mex.
> Can.

Scot.
Ger.
Gt. Brit.
U.S. *or* US
U.S.S.R. *or* USSR
U.K. *or* UK
U.A.E. *or* UAE

23. *United States* is often abbreviated when it is being used as an adjective, such as when it modifies the name of a federal agency, policy, or program. When *United States* is used as a noun in running text, it is usually spelled out, or it is spelled on its initial use and then abbreviated in subsequent references.

U.S. Department of Justice
U.S. foreign policy
The United States has offered to . . .

24. *Saint* is usually abbreviated when it is part of the name of a geographical or topographical feature. *Mount, Point,* and *Fort* are variously spelled out or abbreviated according to individual preference. *Saint, Mount* and *Point* are routinely abbreviated when space is at a premium. (For more on the abbreviation of *Saint,* see paragraph 36 below.)

St. Louis, Missouri
St. Kitts
Mount McKinley
Mount St. Helens
Fort Sumter
Point Pelee

Latin Words and Phrases—See also **Footnotes** above.

25. Words and phrases derived from Latin are commonly abbreviated in contexts where readers can reasonably be expected to recognize them. They are punctuated, not capitalized, and usually not italicized.

etc.
i.e.
e.g.
viz.
et al.
pro tem.

Latitude and Longitude

26. Latitude and longitude are abbreviated in tabular data but written out in running text.

in a table
lat. 10°20′N *or* lat. 10-20N

in text
from 10°20′ north latitude to 10°30′ south latitude

Laws and Bylaws

27. Laws and bylaws, when first mentioned, are spelled in full; however, subsequent references to them in a text may be abbreviated.

first reference   Article I, Section 1
subsequent reference   Art. I, Sec. 1

Military Ranks and Units

28. Military ranks are usually given in full when used with a surname only but are abbreviated when used with a full name.

Colonel Howe
Col. John P. Howe

29. In nonmilitary publications, abbreviations for military ranks are punctuated and set in capital and lowercase letters. Within the military (with the exception of the Marine Corps) these abbreviations are all-capitalized and unpunctuated. The Marine Corps follows the punctuated, capital and lowercase styling.

in the military	BG John T. Dow, USA
	LCDR Mary I. Lee, USN
	Col. S. J. Smith, USMC
outside the military	Brig. Gen. John T. Dow, USA
	Lt. Comdr. Mary I. Lee, USN
	Col. S. J. Smith, USMC

30. Abbreviations for military units are capitalized and unpunctuated.

> USA
> USAF
> SAC
> NORAD

Number

31. The word *number,* when used with figures such as *1* or *2* to indicate a rank or rating, is usually abbreviated. When it is, the *N* is capitalized, and the abbreviation is punctuated.

> The No. 1 priority is to promote profitability.

32. The word *number* is usually abbreviated when it is part of a set unit (as a contract number), when it is used in tabular data, or when it is used in bibliographic references.

Contract No. N-1234-76-57
Publ. Nos. 12 and 13
Policy No. 123-5-X
Index No. 7855

Period with Abbreviations—See section on Punctuation above.

Personal Names

33. First names are not usually abbreviated.

George S. Patterson   *not*   Geo. S. Patterson

34. Unspaced initials of famous persons are sometimes used in place of their full names. The initials may or may not be punctuated.

FDR   *or*   F.D.R.

35. When initials are used with a surname, they are spaced and punctuated.

F. D. Roosevelt

Plurals—See section on Plurals, Possessives, and Compounds above.

Possessives—See section on Plurals, Possessives, and Compounds above.

Saint

36. The word *Saint* is often abbreviated when used before the name of a saint or when it is the first element of the name of a city or institution named after a saint. However, when it forms part of a surname, it may or may not be abbreviated. In the case of surnames and names of institutions, the styling should be the one used by the person or the institution.

St. Peter   *or*   Saint Peter
St. Cloud, Minnesota
St. John's University
Saint Joseph College
Ruth St. Denis
Louis St. Laurent
Augustus Saint-Gaudens

Scientific Terms—See also **Units of Measure** below.

37. In binomial nomenclature, a genus name is usually abbreviated with its initial letter after the first reference to it is spelled out. The abbreviation is always punctuated.

first reference   *Escherichia coli*
subsequent reference   *E. coli*

38. Abbreviations for the names of chemical compounds or mechanical or electronic equipment or processes are usually not punctuated.

OCR
PCB
CPU
PBX

39. The symbols for chemical elements are not punctuated.

H
Cl
Pb
Na

Time—See also **A.D. and B.C.** and **Dates** above and **Units of Measure** below.

40. When time is expressed in figures, the abbreviations that follow are most often styled as punctuated lowercase letters; punctuated small capital letters are also common.

> 8:30 a.m.
> 10:00 p.m.
> 8:30 A.M.
> 10:00 P.M.

41. In transportation schedules *a.m.* and *p.m.* are generally styled in capitalized, unpunctuated, unspaced letters.

> 8:30 AM
> 10:00 PM

42. Time zone designations are usually styled in capitalized, unpunctuated, unspaced letters.

> EST
> PST
> CDT

Titles—See also **Degrees** and **Military Ranks and Units** above.

43. The only courtesy titles that are invariably abbreviated in written references are *Mr., Ms., Mrs.,* and

Messrs. Other titles, such as *Doctor, Representative,* or *Senator,* may be either written out or abbreviated.

> Ms. Lee A. Downs
> Messrs. Lake, Mason, and Nambeth
> Doctor Howe *or* Dr. Howe
> Senator Long *or* Sen. Long

44. Despite some traditional injunctions against the practice, the titles *Honorable* and *Reverend* are often abbreviated when used with *the.*

> the Honorable Samuel I. O'Leary *or* the Hon. Samuel I. O'Leary
> the Reverend Samuel I. O'Leary *or* the Rev. Samuel I. O'Leary

NOTE: There is also a traditional injunction against using the titles *Honorable* and *Reverend* without *the* preceding them. However, in current practice, *Reverend* and *Rev.* are commonly used without *the.*

> the Reverend Samuel I. O'Leary *or*   Rev. Samuel I. O'Leary

45. The designations *Jr.* and *Sr.* may be used in conjunction with courtesy titles, with abbreviations for academic degrees, and with professional rating abbreviations. They may or may not be preceded by a comma according to the writer's preference. They are terminated with a period, and they are commonly only used with a full name.

> Mr. John K. Walker, Jr.
> Dr. John K. Walker, Jr.

General John K. Walker Jr.
The Honorable John K. Walker, Jr.
John K. Walker Jr., M.D.

46. When an abbreviation for an academic degree, professional certification, or association membership follows a name, it is usually preceded by a comma. No courtesy title should precede the name.

Dr. John Smith *or* John Smith, M.D. *but not* Dr. John Smith, M.D.
Katherine Derwinski, CLU
Carol Manning, M.D., FACPS

47. The abbreviation *Esq.* for *Esquire* is used in the United States after the surname of professional persons such as attorneys, architects, consuls, clerks of the court, and justices of the peace. It is not used, however, if *the Honorable* precedes the first name. If a courtesy title such as *Dr., Hon., Miss, Mr., Mrs.,* or *Ms.* is used in correspondence, *Esq.* is omitted. *Esquire* or *Esq.* is frequently used in the United States after the surname of a woman lawyer, although the practice has not yet gained acceptance in all law offices or among all state bar associations.

Carolyn B. West, Esq.

Units of Measure

48. Measures and weights may be abbreviated in figure plus unit combinations; however, if the numeral is written out, the unit should also be written out.

15 cu ft   *or*   15 cu. ft.   *but*   fifteen cubic feet
How many cubic feet does the refrigerator hold?

49. Abbreviations for metric units are usually not punctuated. In many scientific and technical publications, abbreviations for traditional nonmetric units are also unpunctuated. However, in most general-interest publications, abbreviations for traditional units are punctuated.

14 ml
12 km
22 mi.
8 ft.
4 sec.
20 min.

Versus

50. *Versus* is abbreviated as the lowercase roman letter *v.* in legal contexts; it is either spelled out or abbreviated as lowercase roman letters *vs.* in general contexts.

in a legal context   Smith v. *Vermont*
in a general context   honesty versus dishonesty
                             or
                          honesty vs. dishonesty

Chapter 5

The Treatment of Numbers

CONTENTS

The styling of numbers presents special difficulties to writers and editors because there are so many conventions to follow, some of which may conflict when applied to particular passages. The writer's major decision is whether to write out numbers in running text or to express them in figures. Usage varies considerably, in part because no single neat formula covers all the categories in which numbers are used. In general, the more formal the writing the more likely that numbers will be spelled out. In scientific, technical, or statistical contexts, however, numbers are likely to be expressed as figures. This chapter explains most of the conventions used in the styling of numbers. A discussion of general principles is followed by detailed information on specific situations involving numbers.

Numbers as Words or Figures

At one extreme of styling, all numbers, sometimes even including dates, are written out. This usage is uncommon and is usually limited to proclamations, legal documents, and some other types of very formal writing. This styling is space-consuming and time-consuming; it can also be ungainly or, worse, unclear. At the other extreme, some types of technical writing, such as statistical reports, contain no written-out numbers except at the beginning of a sentence.

In general, figures are easier to read than the spelled-out forms of numbers; however, the spelled-out forms are helpful in certain circumstances, such as in distinguishing different categories of numbers or in providing relief from an overwhelming cluster of numerals. Most writers follow one or the other of two common conventions combining numerals and written-out numbers. The conventions are described in this section, along with the situations that provide exceptions to the general rules.

Basic Conventions

1. The first system requires that a writer use figures for exact numbers that are greater than nine and words for numbers nine and below (a variation of this system sets the number ten as the dividing point). In this system, numbers that consist of a whole number between one and nine followed by *hundred, thousand, million,* etc. may be spelled out or expressed in figures.

She has performed in 22 plays on Broadway, seven of which won Pulitzer prizes.

The new edition will consist of 25 volumes which will be issued at a rate of approximately four volumes per year.

The cat show attracted an unexpected two thousand entries.

They sold more than 2,000 units in the first year.

2. The second system requires that a writer use figures for all exact numbers 100 and above (or 101 and above) and words for numbers from one to ninety-nine (or one to one hundred) and for numbers that consist of a whole number between one and ninety-nine followed by *hundred, thousand, million,* etc.

The artist spent nearly twelve years completing these four volumes, which comprise 435 hand-colored engravings.

The 145 participants in the seminar toured the area's eighteen period houses.

In the course of four hours, the popular author signed twenty-five hundred copies of her new book.

Sentence Beginnings

3. Numbers that begin a sentence are written out, although some make an exception for the use of figures for dates that begin a sentence. Most writers, however, try to avoid spelled-out numbers that are lengthy and awkward by restructuring the sentence so that the number appears elsewhere than at the beginning and may then be styled as a figure.

Sixty-two species of Delphinidae inhabit the world's oceans.

or

The Delphinidae consist of 62 ocean-dwelling species.

Twelve fifteen was the year King John of England signed the Magna Carta.

or

1215 was the year King John of England signed the Magna Carta.

or

In 1215 King John of England signed the Magna Carta.

One hundred fifty-seven illustrations, including 86 color plates, are contained in the book.

or

The book contains 157 illustrations, including 86 color plates.

Adjacent Numbers and Numbers in Series

4. Generally, two separate sets of figures should not be written adjacent to one another in running text unless they form a series. So that the juxtaposition of unrelated figures will not confuse the reader, either the sentence is restructured or one of the figures is spelled out. Usually the figure with the written form that is shorter and more easily read is converted. When one of two adjacent numbers is an element of a compound modifier, the first of the two numbers is often expressed in words, the second in figures. But if the second number is the shorter, the styling is often reversed.

original	*change to*
16 ½-inch dowels	sixteen ½-inch dowels
25 11-inch platters	twenty-five 11-inch platters

20 100-point games	twenty 100-point games
78 20-point games	78 twenty-point games
By 1997, 300 more of the state's schools will have closed their doors.	By 1997, three hundred more of the state's schools will have closed their doors.

5. Numbers paired at the beginning of a sentence are usually styled alike. If the first word of the sentence is a spelled-out number, the second, related number is also spelled out. However, some writers and editors prefer that each number be styled independently, even if that results in an inconsistent pairing.

> Sixty to seventy-five acres were destroyed.
> Sixty to 75 acres were destroyed.

6. Numbers that form a pair or a series referring to comparable quantities within a sentence or a paragraph should be treated consistently. The style of the largest number usually determines the style of the other numbers. Thus, a series of numbers including some which would ordinarily be spelled out might all be styled as figures. Similarly, figures are used to express all the numbers in a series if one of those numbers is a mixed or simple fraction.

> Graduating from the obedience class were 3 corgis, 20 Doberman pinschers, 19 German shepherds, 9 golden retrievers, 10 Labrador retrievers, and 1 Rottweiler.
> The three jobs took 5, 12, and 4½ hours, respectively.

Round Numbers

7. Approximate or round numbers, particularly those
   that can be expressed in one or two words, are often written out in general writing; in technical and
   scientific writing they are more likely to be expressed as numerals.

   > seven hundred people
   > five thousand years
   > four hundred thousand volumes
   > seventeen thousand metric tons
   > four hundred million dollars
   > *but in technical writing*
   > 50,000 people per year
   > 20,000 species of fish

8. For easier reading, numbers of one million and
   above may be expressed as figures followed by the
   word *million, billion,* and so forth. The figure may
   include a decimal fraction, but the fraction is not
   usually carried past the first digit to the right of the
   decimal point, and it is never carried past the third
   digit. If a more exact number is required, the
   whole amount should be written in figures.

   > about 4.6 billion years old
   > 1.2 million metric tons of grain
   > the last 600 million years
   > $7.25 million
   > $3,456,000,000
   > *but* 200,000 years   *not*   200 thousand years

NOTE: In the United Kingdom, the word *billion*
refers to an amount that in the United States is
called *trillion.* In the American system each of the

denominations above 1,000 millions (the American billion) is one thousand times the one preceding (thus, one trillion equals 1,000 billions; one quadrillion equals 1,000 trillions). In the British system the first denomination above 1,000 millions (the British milliard) is one thousand times the preceding one, but each of the denominations above 1,000 milliards (the British billion) is one million times the preceding one (thus, one trillion equals 1,000,000 billions; one quadrillion equals 1,000,000 trillions).

Ordinal Numbers

1. Ordinal numbers generally follow the styling rules for cardinal numbers that are listed above in the section on Numbers as Words or Figures: if a figure would be required for the cardinal form of a number, it should also be used for the ordinal form; if conventions call for a written-out form, it should be used for both cardinal and ordinal numbers. In technical writing, however, as well as in footnotes and tables, all ordinal numbers are written as figure-plus-suffix combinations. In addition, certain ordinal numbers—those specifying percentiles and latitudinal lines are common ones—are conventionally set as figures in both general and technical writing.

the sixth Robert de Bruce
the 20th century
the ninth grade
the 98th Congress
the 9th and 14th chapters
the 12th percentile
his twenty-third try
the 40th parallel

2. The forms *second* and *third* may be written with figures as *2d* or *2nd*, *3d* or *3rd*, *22d* or *22nd*, *93d* or *93rd*, *102d* or *102nd*. A period does not follow the suffix.

Roman Numerals

Roman numerals, which may be written either in capital or lowercase letters, are conventional in the specific situations described below. Roman numerals are formed by adding the numerical values of letters as they are arranged in descending order going from left to right. If a letter with a smaller numerical value is placed to the left of a letter with a greater numerical value, the value of the smaller is subtracted from the value of the larger. A bar placed over a numeral ($\bar{V}$) multiplies its value by one thousand. A list of Roman numerals and their Arabic equivalents is given in the table on pages 297–298.

1. Roman numerals are traditionally used to differentiate rulers and popes that have identical names.

Elizabeth II
Innocent X
Henry VIII
Louis XIV

2. Roman numerals are used to differentiate related males who have the same name. The numerals are used only with a person's full name and, unlike the similar forms *Junior* and *Senior*, they are placed after the surname with no intervening comma. Ordinals are sometimes used instead of Roman numerals.

James R. Watson II
James R. Watson 2nd *or* 2d
James R. Watson III
James R. Watson 3rd *or* 3d
James R. Watson IV
James R. Watson 4th

NOTE: Possessive patterns for these names are the following:

singular
James R. Watson III's (*or* 3rd's *or* 3d's) house
plural
the James R. Watson IIIs' (*or* 3rds' *or* 3ds') house

3. Roman numerals are used to differentiate certain vehicles and vessels, such as yachts, that have the same name. If the name is italicized, the numeral is italicized also. Names of American spacecraft formerly bore Roman numerals, but Arabic numerals are now used.

Shamrock V

The U.S. spacecraft *Rangers VII, VIII,* and *IX* took pictures of the moon.

On July 20, 1969, *Apollo 11* landed on the moon.

4. Lowercase Roman numerals are often used to number book pages that precede the regular Arabic sequence, as in a foreword, preface, or introduction.

5. Roman numerals are often used in enumerations to list major headings. An example of an outline with Roman-numeral headings is shown on page 240.

6. Roman numerals are sometimes used to specify a particular act and scene of a play or a particular volume in a collection. In this system, capitalized Roman numerals are used for the number of the act, and lowercase Roman numerals for the number of the scene. Arabic numerals are increasingly used for these purposes, however.

Roman style
Richard II, Act II, scene i
Hamlet, I.i.63
II, iii, 13-20

Arabic style
Act 2, scene 1
Act 1, scene 1, line 63 *or* 1.1.63
2, 3, 13-20

7. Roman numerals are found as part of a few estab-

lished technical terms such as blood-clotting factors, quadrant numbers, and designations of cra-
nial nerves. Also, chords in the study of music
harmony are designated by capital and lowercase
Roman numerals. For the most part, however,
technical terms that include numbers express them
in Arabic form.

> blood-clotting factor VII
> quadrant III
> the cranial nerves II, IV, and IX
> Population II stars
> type I error
> > *but*
> adenosine 3′, 5′-monophosphate
> cesium 137
> PL/1 programming language

Punctuation, Spacing, and Inflection

This section explains general rules for the use of commas, hyphens, and spacing in compound and large
numbers, as well as the plural forms of numbers. For
the styling of specific categories of numbers, such as
dates, money, and decimal fractions, see the section on
Specific Styling Conventions in this chapter.

Commas and Spaces in Large Numbers

1. In general writing, with the exceptions explained
   in paragraph 3 below, figures of four digits may be

styled with or without a comma; the punctuated form is more common. In scientific writing, these numerals are usually styled with a comma (but see paragraph 4 below). If the numerals form part of a tabulation, commas are necessary so that four-digit numerals can align with numerals of five or more digits.

2,000 case histories   *or less commonly*   1253 people

2. Whole numbers of five digits or more (but not decimal fractions) use a comma or a space to separate three-digit groups, counting from the right. Commas are used in general writing; either spaces or commas are used in technical writing.

a fee of $12,500
15,000 units   *or*   15 000 units
a population of 1,500,000   *or*   1 500 000

3. Certain types of numbers do not conform to these conventions. Decimal fractions and serial and multidigit numbers in set combinations, such as the numbers of policies, contracts, checks, streets, rooms, suites, telephones, pages, military hours, and years, do not contain commas. Numerals used in binary notation are also written without commas or spaces.

check 34567
the year 1929
page 209
Policy No. 33442
Room 606
10011

1650 hours
111010

NOTE: Year numbers of five or more digits (as geological or archeological dates) do contain a comma.

The Wisconsin glaciation lasted from approximately 70,000 to 10,000 years B.P.

4. In technical and scientific writing, lengthy figures are usually avoided by the use of special units of measure and by the use of multipliers and powers of ten. When long figures are written, however, each group of three digits may be separated by a space counting from the decimal point to the left and the right. If the digits are separated by a comma instead of a space, neither commas nor spaces are placed to the right of the decimal point. Whichever system is used should be applied consistently to all numbers with four or more digits.

27 483 241
27,483,241
23.000 003
23.000003
27 483.241 755
27,483.241755

Hyphens

5. Hyphens are used with written-out numbers between 21 and 99.

forty-one
forty-first

four hundred twenty-two
the twenty-fifth day

6. A hyphen is used between the numerator and the
   denominator of a fraction that is written out when
   that fraction is used as a modifier. A written-out
   fraction consisting of two words only (as *two thirds*)
   is usually styled open, although the hyphenated
   form is common also. Multiword numerators and
   denominators are usually hyphenated. If either the
   numerator or the denominator is hyphenated, no
   hyphen is used between them. For more on fractions, see pages 240–242.

   a two-thirds majority of the staff
   three fifths of her paycheck
   seven and four fifths
   forty-five hundredths
   four five-hundredths

7. Numbers that form the first part of a compound
   modifier expressing measurement are followed by
   a hyphen. An exception to this practice is that
   numbers are not followed by a hyphen when the
   second part of the modifier is the word *percent*.

   a 5-foot board
   an eight-pound baby
   a 28-mile trip
   a 680-acre ranch
   a 10-pound weight
   a 75 percent reduction

8. An adjective or adverb made from a numeral plus
   the suffix *-fold* contains a hyphen, while a similar

term made from a written-out number is styled solid. (For more on the use of suffixes with numbers, see page 184 in Chapter 3, "Plurals, Possessives, and Compounds.")

> a fourfold increase
> increased 20-fold

9. Serial numbers, such as social security or engine numbers, often contain hyphens that make lengthy numerals more readable.

> 020-42-1691

10. Numbers are usually not divided at the end of a line. If division is unavoidable, the break occurs only after a comma. End-of-line breaks do not occur at decimal points, and a name with a numerical suffix (as *Elizabeth II*) is not divided between the name and the numeral.

Inclusive Numbers

11. Inclusive numbers—those which express a range— are separated either by the word *to* or by an en dash, which serves as an arbitrary equivalent of the phrase "(up) to and including" when used between dates and other inclusive numbers. (The en dash is explained further in the section on Dash, beginning on page 42, in Chapter 1, "Punctuation.") En dashes are used in tables, parenthetical references, and footnotes to save space. In running text, however, the word *to* is more often used.

> pages 40 to 98
> the years 1960–1965

pages 40–98
spanning the years 1915 to 1941
pp. 40–98
the decade 1920–1930
14–18 months
the fiscal year 1984–1985

NOTE: Inclusive numbers separated by an en dash are not used in combination with the words *from* or *between,* as in "from 1955–60" or "between 1970–90." Instead, phrases like these are written as "from 1955 to 1960" or "between 1970 and 1990."

12. Units of measurement expressed in words or abbreviations are usually used only after the second element of an inclusive number. Symbols, however, are repeated.

> an increase in dosage from 200 to 500 mg
> running 50 to 75 miles every week
> ten to fifteen dollars
> 30 to 35 degrees Celsius
> > *but*
> $50 to $60 million
> 45° to 48° F
> 45°–48°
> 3'–5' long

13. Numbers that are part of an inclusive set or range are usually styled alike: figures with figures, spelled-out words with other spelled-out words. Similarly, approximate numbers are usually not paired with exact numbers.

> from 8 to 108 absences
> five to twenty guests
> 300,000 to 305,000 *not* 300 thousand to 305,000

14. Inclusive page numbers and dates that use the en dash may be written in full (1981–1982) or elided (1981–82). Both stylings are widely used. However, inclusive dates that appear in titles and other headings are almost never elided. Dates that appear with era designations are also not elided.

NOTE: Elided numbers are commonly used because they save space, but the principles governing their use must be understood and followed consistently. The most frequently used style for the elision of inclusive numbers is based on the following rules:

1. Never elide inclusive numbers that have only two digits: 33-37, *not* 33–7.
2. Never elide inclusive numbers when the first number ends in 00: 100–108, *not* 100–08 *and not* 100–8.
3. In other numbers, omit *only* the hundreds digit from the higher number: 232–34, *not* 232–4.
4. Where the next-to-last digit of both numbers is zero, write only one digit for the higher number: 103–4, *not* 103–04.

> 467–68   *or*   467–468
> 1724–27   *or*   1724–1727
> 550–602
> 1463–1510
> 203–4   *or*   203–204
> 1800–1801
> 552–549 B.C.

Plurals

15. The plurals of written-out numbers are formed by the addition of -*s* or -*es*.

Back in the thirties these roads were unpaved.

Christmas shoppers bought the popular toy in twos and threes.

16. The plurals of figures are formed by adding -*s*. Some writers and publications prefer to add an apostrophe before the -*s*. For more on the plurals of figures, see the section on Plurals, beginning on page 140, in Chapter 3, "Plurals, Possessives, and Compounds," and the section on Apostrophe, beginning on page 7, in Chapter 1, "Punctuation."

This ghost town was booming back in the 1840s.

The first two artificial hearts to be implanted in human patients were Jarvik-7s.

but also
linen manufacture in France in the 1700's

1's and *7*'s that looked alike

Specific Styling Conventions

The following paragraphs describe styling practices commonly followed for specific types of situations involving numbers. The paragraphs are arranged under the following alphabetical headings:

Addresses
Dates
Degrees of Temperature and Arc
Enumerations and Outlines
Fractions and Decimal Fractions

Money
Percentages
Proper Names
Ratios
Serial Numbers and Miscellaneous Numbers
Time of Day
Units of Measurement

Addresses

1. Arabic numerals are used for all building, house, apartment, room, and suite numbers except for *one*, which is written out.

   6 Lincoln Road
   1436 Fremont Street
   Apt. 281, Regency Park Drive
   Room 617, McClaskey Building
       but
   One Bayside Drive
   One World Trade Center

   NOTE: When the address of a building is used as its name, the number in the address is written out.

   Fifty Maple Street

2. Numbered streets have their numbers written as ordinals. There are two distinct conventions for the styling of numbered street names. The first, useful where space is limited, calls for Arabic numerals to denote all numbered streets above Twelfth; numbered street names from First through Twelfth are written out. A second, more formal, convention calls for the writing out of all numbered street names up to and including One Hundredth.

19 South 22nd Street
145 East 145th Street
167 West Second Avenue
122 East Forty-second Street
One East Ninth Street
36 East Fiftieth
in the Sixties (streets from 60th to 69th)
in the 120s (streets from 120th to 129th)

NOTE: A disadvantage of the first convention is that the direct juxtaposition of the house or building number and the street number may occur when there is no intervening word such as a compass direction. In these cases, a spaced hyphen or en dash may be inserted to distinguish the two numbers, or the second convention may be used and the street number written out.

2018–14th Street
2018 Fourteenth Street

3. Arabic numerals are used to designate interstate, federal, and state highways and, in some states, county roads.

U.S. Route 1   *or*   U.S. 1
Interstate 91   *or*   I-91
Massachusetts 57
Indiana 60
County 213

Dates

4. Year numbers are styled as figures. However, if a number representing a year begins a sentence, it may be written in full or the sentence rewritten to avoid beginning it with a figure. (For additional examples, see paragraph 3 in the section on Numbers as Words or Figures in this chapter.)

> in 323 B.C.
> before A.D. 40
> 1888–96
> Fifteen eighty-eight marked the end to Spanish ambitions for the control of England.
> *or*
> Spanish ambitions for the control of England ended in 1588 with the destruction of their "Invincible Armada."

5. A year number may be abbreviated, or cut back to its last two digits, in informal writing or when an event is so well-known that it needs no century designation. In these cases an apostrophe precedes the numerals. For more on this use of the apostrophe, see the section on Apostrophe, beginning on page 7, in Chapter 1, "Punctuation."

> He always maintained that he'd graduated from Korea, Clash of '52.
> the blizzard of '88

6. Full dates (month, day, and year) may be styled in one of two distinct patterns. The traditional styling is the month-day-year sequence, with the year set off by commas that precede and follow it. An alternate styling is the inverted date, or day-month-year sequence, which does not require commas. This sequence is used in Great Britain, in U.S. government publications, and in the military.

traditional style
July 8, 1776, was a warm, sunny day in Philadelphia.
the explosion on July 16, 1945, at Alamogordo

military style
the explosion on 16 July 1945 at Alamogordo
Lee's surrender to Grant on 9 April 1865 at Appomattox

7. Ordinal numbers are not used in expressions of full dates. Even though the numbers may be pronounced as ordinals, they are written as cardinal numbers. Ordinals may be used, however, to express a date without an accompanying year, and they are always used when preceded in a date by the word *the*.

> December 4, 1829
> on December 4th   *or*   on December 4
> on the 4th of December
> on the 4th

8. Commas are usually omitted from dates that include the month and year but not the day. Alternatively, writers sometimes insert the word *of* between month and year.

> in November 1805
> back in January of 1981

9. Once a numerical date has been given, a reference to a related date may be written out.

> After the rioting of August 3 the town was quiet, and by the seventh most troops had been pulled out.

10. All-figure dating (as 6-8-85 or 6/8/85) is inappro-

priate except in the most informal writing. It also creates a problem of ambiguity, as it may mean either June 8, 1985, or August 6, 1985.

11. References to specific centuries are often written out, although they may be expressed in figures, especially when they form the first element of a compound modifier.

> the nineteenth century
> a sixteenth-century painting
> > *but also*
> a 12th-century illuminated manuscript
> 20th-century revolutions

12. In general writing, the name of a specific decade often takes a short form. Although many writers place an apostrophe before the shortened word and a few capitalize it, both the apostrophe and the capitalization are often omitted when the context clearly indicates that a date is being referred to.

> in the turbulent seventies
> growing up in the thirties
> > *but also*
> back in the 'forties
> in the early Fifties

13. The name of a specific decade is often expressed in numerals, usually in plural form. (For more on the formation of plural numbers, see paragraphs 1 and 2 in the section on Punctuation, Spacing, and Inflection in this chapter.) The figure may be shortened with an apostrophe to indicate the missing numerals, but any sequence of such numbers should be styled consistently. (For more on this use of the apostrophe, see the section on Apostrophe, beginning on page 7, in Chapter 1, "Punctuation.")

> during the 1920s   *or*   during the 1920's
> the 1950s and 1960s   *or*   the '50s and '60s
>   *but not*
> the 1950s and '60s
> the 1930s and forties
>   *and not*
> the '50's and '60's

14. Era designations precede or follow words that specify centuries or numerals that specify years. Era designations are unspaced and are nearly always abbreviated; they are usually printed as small capitals and typed as regular capitals, and they may or may not be punctuated with periods. Any date that is given without an era designation or context is understood to mean A.D. The two most commonly used abbreviations are B.C. (before Christ) and A.D. (*anno Domini*, "in the year of our Lord"). The abbreviation B.C. is placed after the date, while A.D. is usually placed before the date but after a century designation. (For more on the use of these abbreviations, see pages 195–196 of Chapter 4, "Abbreviations.")

> 1792–1750 B.C.
> between 600 and 400 B.C.
> from the fifth or fourth millennium to c. 250 B.C.
> 35,000 B.C.
> between 7 B.C. and A.D. 22
> c. A.D. 1100
> the second century A.D.
> the seventeenth century

15. Less commonly used era designations include A.H. (*anno Hegirae*, "in the year of [Muhammad's] Hegira," or *anno Hebraico*, "in the Hebrew year"); B.C.E. (before the common era; a synonym for B.C.); C.E.(of the common era; a synonym for A.D.); and B.P. (before the present; often used by geologists and archaeologists, with or without the word *year*). The abbreviation A.H. in both its meanings is usually placed before the year number, while B.C.E., C.E., and B.P. are placed after it.

> the tenth of Muharram, A.H. 61 (October 10, A.D. 680)
> the first century A.H.
> from the first century B.C.E. to the fourth century C.E.
> 63 B.C.E.
> the year 200 C.E.
> 5,000 years B.P.
> two million years B.P.

Degrees of Temperature and Arc

16. In technical writing, figures are generally used for quantities expressed in degrees. In addition, the degree symbol (°) rather than the word *degree* is used with the figure. With the Kelvin scale, however, neither the word *degree* nor the symbol is used with the figure.

> a 45° angle
> 6°40′10″N
> 32° F
> 0° C
> Absolute zero is zero kelvins or 0 K.

NOTE: In some technical and scientific publications, the degree symbol and the *F* or *C* that may follow it are always written without any space between them. Another style followed in some scientific publications is to omit the degree symbol in expressions of temperature.

> 100°F   *or*   100F
> 39°C   *or*   39C

17. In general writing the quantity expressed in degrees may or may not be written out, depending upon the styling conventions being followed. In general, a figure is followed by the degree symbol or the word *degree*; a written-out number is always followed by the word *degree*.

> latitude 43°19″ N
> latitude 43 degrees N
> a difference of 43 degrees latitude
> The temperature has risen thirty degrees since this morning.

Enumerations and Outlines

18. Both run-in and vertical enumerations are often numbered. In run-in enumerations, each item is preceded by a number (or an italicized letter) enclosed in parentheses. The items in the list are separated by commas if the items are brief and have little or no internal punctuation; if the items are complex, they are separated by semicolons. The entire run-in enumeration is introduced by a colon if it is preceded by a full clause.

> We feel that she should (1) increase her administrative skills, (2) pursue additional professional education, and (3) increase her production.

The oldest and most basic word-processing systems consist of the following: (1) a typewriter for keyboarding information, (2) a console to house the storage medium, and (3) the medium itself.

The vendor of your system should (1) instruct you in the care and maintenance of your system; (2) offer regularly scheduled maintenance to ensure that the system is clean, with lubrication and replacement of parts as necessary; and (3) respond promptly to service calls.

19. In vertical enumerations, the numbers are usually not enclosed in parentheses but are followed by a period. Each item in the enumeration begins its own line, which is either flush left or indented. Runover lines are usually aligned with the first word that follows the number, and figures are aligned on the periods that follow them. Each item on the list is usually capitalized if the items on the list are syntactically independent of the words that introduce them; however, style varies on this point, and use of a lowercase style for such items is fairly common. There is no terminal punctuation following the items unless at least one of the items is a complete sentence, in which case a period follows each item. Items that are syntactically dependent on the words that introduce them begin with a lowercase letter and carry the same punctuation marks that they would if they were a run-in series in a sentence.

Required skills include the following:
1. Shorthand
2. Typing
3. Transcription

To type a three-column table, follow this procedure:
1. Clear tab stops.
2. Remove margin stops.
3. Determine precise center of the page. Set a tab stop at center.

The vendor of your system should
1. instruct you in the care and maintenance of your system;
2. offer regularly scheduled maintenance to ensure that the system is clean, with lubrication and replacement parts as necessary; and
3. respond promptly to service calls.

20. Outlines make use of Roman numerals, Arabic numerals, and letters.

I. Editorial tasks
  A. Manuscript editing
  B. Author contact
    1. Authors already under contract
    2. New authors
II. Production responsibilities
  A. Scheduling
    1. Composition
    2. Printing and binding
  B. Cost estimates and bids
    1. Composition
    2. Printing and binding

Fractions and Decimal Fractions

21. In running text, fractions standing alone are usually written out. Common fractions used as nouns are usually styled as open compounds, but when they are used as modifiers they are usually hyphenated. For more on written-out fractions, see page 226.

> two thirds of the paint
> a two-thirds majority
> three thirty-seconds
> seventy-two hundredths
> one one-hundredth

NOTE: Most writers try to find ways to avoid the necessity of writing out complicated fractions (as *forty-two seventy-fifths*).

22. Mixed fractions (fractions with a whole number, such as 3½) and fractions that form part of a unit modifier are expressed in figures in running text. A *-th* is not added to a figure fraction.

> waiting 2½ hours
> a ⅞-mile course
> 1¼ million population
> a 2½-kilometer race

NOTE: When mixed fractions are typewritten, the typist leaves a space between the whole number and the fraction. The space is closed up when the number is set in print. Fractions that are not on the typewriter keyboard may be made up by typing the numerator, a virgule, and the denominator in succession without spacing.

23. Fractions used with units of measurement are expressed in figures.

> ¹⁄₁₀ km
> ¼ mile

24. Decimal fractions are always set as figures. In technical writing, a zero is placed to the left of the decimal point when the fraction is less than a whole number. In general writing, the zero is usually omitted.

> An example of a pure decimal fraction is 0.375, while 1.402 is classified as a mixed decimal fraction.
> 0.142857
> 0.2 gm
> received 0.1 mg/kg diazepam i.v.
> *but*
> a .40 gauge shotgun

25. A comma is never inserted in the numbers following a decimal point, although spaces may be inserted as described and illustrated in paragraph 4 in the section on Punctuation, Spacing, and Inflection in this chapter.

26. Fractions and decimal fractions are usually not mixed in a text.

> 5½ lb. 2⅕ oz.
> 5.5 lb. 2.2 oz.
> *but not*
> 5½ lb. 2.2 oz.

Money

27. Sums of money are expressed in words or figures, according to the conventions described in the first section of this chapter. If the sum can be expressed in one or two words, it is usually written out in running text. But if several sums are mentioned in the sentence or paragraph, all are usually expressed as figures. When the amount is written out, the unit of currency is also written out. If the sum is expressed in figures, the symbol of the currency unit is used, with no space between it and the numerals.

> We paid $175,000 for the house.
> My change came to 87¢.
> The shop charged $67.50 for hand-knit sweaters.
> The price of a nickel candy bar seems to have risen to more like forty cents.
> Fifty dollars was stolen from my wallet.
> forty thousand dollars
> fifty-two dollars

28. Monetary units of mixed dollars-and-cents amounts are expressed in figures.

> $16.75
> $307.02
> $1.95

29. Even-dollar amounts are often expressed in figures without a decimal point and zeros. But when even-dollar amounts are used in a series with or are near to amounts that include dollars and cents, the decimal point and zeros are usually added for consistency. The dollar sign is repeated before each amount in a series or inclusive range; the word *dollar* may or may not be repeated.

> The price of the book rose from $7.95 in 1970 to $8.00 in 1971 and then to $8.50 in 1972.

> The bids were eighty, ninety, and one hundred dollars.
>
> *or*
>
> The bids were eighty dollars, one hundred dollars, and three hundred dollars.

30. Sums of money given in round units of millions or above are usually expressed in a combination of figures and words, either with a dollar sign or with the word *dollars*. For more on the handling of round numbers, see paragraphs 7 and 8 in the section on Numbers as Words or Figures in this chapter.

> 60 million dollars
> a $10 million building program
> $4.5 billion

31. In legal documents a sum of money is usually written out fully, with the corresponding figures in parentheses immediately following.

> twenty-five thousand dollars ($25,000)

Percentages

32. In technical writing and in tables and footnotes, specific percentages are styled as figure plus unspaced percent sign (%). In general writing, the percentage number may be expressed as a figure or spelled out, depending upon the conventions that apply to it. The word *percent* rather than the symbol is used in nonscientific texts.

> *technical*
> *15%*
> *13.5%*

general
15 percent
87.2 percent
Twenty-five percent of the office staff was out with
the flu.
a four percent increase

33. The word *percentage* or *percent,* used as a noun without an adjacent numeral, should never be replaced
by a percent sign.

> Only a small percentage of the test animals exhibited
> a growth change.
>
> The clinic treated a greater percentage of outpatients
> this year.

34. In a series or unit combination the percent sign
should be included with all numbers, even if one of
the numbers is zero.

> a variation of 0% to 10%

Proper Names

35. Numbers in the names of religious organizations
and of churches are usually written out in ordinal
form. Names of specific ruling houses and governmental bodies may include ordinals, and these are
written out if they are one hundred or below. A
few ruling houses, however, are traditionally designated by Roman numerals that follow the name.

> First Church of Christ, Scientist
> Third Congregational Church
> Seventh-Day Adventists
> Fifth Republic

Third Reich
First Continental Congress
but
Egyptian tombs from Dynasty XI

36. Names of electoral, judicial, and military units may include ordinal numbers that precede the noun. Numbers of one hundred or below may either be written out or styled as numerals.

> First Congressional District
> Twelfth Precinct
> Ninety-eighth Congress *or* 98th Congress
> Circuit Court of Appeals for the Third Circuit
> United States Eighth Army *or* 8th United States Army
> At H hour, the 32d would drive forward to seize the 77th Division's position southeast of Maeda.
> The assault was led by the 54th Massachusetts, the first black regiment recruited in a free state.

37. Specific branches of labor unions and fraternal organizations are conventionally identified by an Arabic numeral usually placed after the name.

> International Brotherhood of Electrical Workers Local 42
> Elks Lodge No. 61
> Local 98 Operating Engineers

Ratios

38. Ratios expressed in figures use a colon, a hyphen, a virgule, or the word *to* as a means of comparison. Ratios expressed in words use a hyphen, or the word *to*.

a 3:1 chance
odds of 100 to 1
a 6-1 vote
22.4 mi/gal
a ratio of ten to four
a fifty-fifty chance

Serial Numbers and Miscellaneous Numerals

39. Figures are used to refer to things that are numbered serially, such as chapter and page numbers, addresses, years, policy and contract numbers, and so forth.

Serial No. 5274
vol. 5, p. 202
Permit No. 63709
1636 Freemont Street
paragraphs 5–7
Table 16
pages 420–515

40. Figures are also used to express stock market quotations, mathematical calculations, scores, and tabulations.

won by a score of 8 to 2
3⅛ percent bonds
the tally: 322 ayes, 80 nays
$3 \times 15 = 45$

Time of Day

41. In running text the time of day is usually spelled out when expressed in even, half, or quarter hours.

Quitting time is four-thirty.

By half past eleven we were all getting hungry.

We should arrive at a quarter past five.

42. The time of day is also usually spelled out when it is followed by the contraction *o'clock* or when *o'clock* is understood.

I plan to leave here at eight o'clock.

He should be here by four at the latest.

My appointment is at eleven o'clock.
or
My appointment is at 11 o'clock.

43. Figures are used to delineate a precise time.

The patient was discharged at 9:15 in the morning.

Her plane is due in at 3:05 this afternoon.

The program starts at 8:30 in the evening.

44. Figures are also written when the time of day is used in conjunction with the abbreviations *a.m.* *(ante meridiem)* and *p.m.* *(post meridiem)*. The punctuated lowercase styling for these abbreviations is most common, but punctuated small capital letters are also frequently used. These abbreviations should not be used in conjunction with the words *morning* or *evening*; and the word *o'clock* should not be combined with either *a.m.* or *p.m.*

8:30 a.m.   *or*   8:30 A.M.

10:30 p.m.   *or*   10:30 P.M.

8 a.m.   *or*   8 A.M.
but
9:15 in the morning

11:00 in the evening

nine o'clock

NOTE: When twelve o'clock is written, it is often helpful to add the designation *midnight* or *noon*, as *a.m.* and *p.m.* sometimes cause confusion.

twelve o'clock (midnight)
twelve o'clock (noon)

45. For consistency, even-hour times should be expressed with a colon and two zeros, when used in a series or pairing with any odd-hour times.

He came at 7:00 and left at 9:45.

46. The 24-hour clock system—also called military time—uses no punctuation and is expressed without the use of *a.m., p.m.,* or *o'clock*.

from 0930 to 1100
at 1600 hours

Units of Measurement

47. In technical writing, numbers used with units of measurement—even numbers below ten—are expressed as numerals.

2 liters
12 miles
55 pounds
6 hectares
60 watts
15 cubic centimeters
20 kilometers
35 milligrams

48. General writing, on the other hand, usually treats these numbers according to the basic conventions explained in the first section of this chapter. However, in some cases writers achieve greater clarity by styling all numbers—even those below ten—that express quantities of physical measurement as numerals.

> The car was traveling in excess of 80 miles an hour.
>
> The old volume weighed three pounds and was difficult to hold in a reading position.
>
> *but also in some general texts*
> 3 hours, 25 minutes
> saw 18 eagles in 12 minutes
> a 6-pound hammer
> weighed 3 pounds, 5 ounces

49. When units of measurement are written as abbreviations or symbols, the adjacent numbers are always figures, in both general and technical texts.

> 6 cm
> 67.6 fl oz
> 1 mm
> 4'
> 10 cm³
> 98.6°
> 3 kg
> $4.25

50. When two or more quantities are expressed, as in ranges or dimensions or series, an accompanying symbol is usually repeated with each figure.

> 2' x 4'
> 4" by 6" cards
> temperature on successive days of 30°, 43°, and 58°
> $400–$500

Chapter 6

Notes and Bibliographies

CONTENTS

Writers and editors often need to provide readers with documentation of the source of a quotation or a piece of information. Authors may also wish to provide additional information and commentary or cross-references. This type of information is usually included in a note, which may take the form of a footnote at the bottom of a page, an endnote at the end of a chapter or at the end of a work, or a note in parentheses.

This chapter describes both the footnote or endnote system and the system of parenthetical references. For both of these systems, the examples in this chapter illustrate generally acceptable ways of styling references; however, writers and editors should be aware that many professions and academic disciplines have developed their own systems for documenting sources, and some of these systems differ from the stylings illustrated in this chapter.

Footnotes and Endnotes

A footnote or an endnote links full bibliographical information about a source, including author, title, place of publication, publisher, date, and page number, to a specific text passage making use of that source. The text passage is marked with a number, and all such notes are set aside from the rest of the text. Notes that appear at the bottom of the page are called *footnotes*. Notes that appear at the end of the chapter or at the end of an entire work are called *endnotes*.

Placement of the Elements

Footnotes and endnotes to a text are indicated by unpunctuated superior Arabic numerals (or reference symbols) placed immediately after the quotation or information with no space in between. The notes should be numbered consecutively, starting with 1, throughout the paper, article, or chapter. The number is usually placed at the end of a sentence or clause, or at some other natural break in the sentence when the reference material is not a quotation. The number follows all marks of punctuation except the dash. If a terminal quotation mark appears (as at the end of a short quotation that is included in the running text), the numeral is placed outside the final quotation mark with no space intervening (see the sample on page 253).

The text of the note itself is introduced with the corresponding Arabic numeral or reference symbol. The numeral may be superior, unpunctuated, and separated from the first word of the footnote by one space,

According to Lesikar, if a "quoted passage is four lines or less in length, it is typed with the report text and is distinguished from the normal text by quotation marks."[17] However, a different procedure is used for longer quotations:

> But if a longer quotation (five lines or more) is used, the conventional practice is to set it in from both left and right margins (about five spaces) but without quotation marks. . . . The quoted passage is further distinguished from the report writer's work by single spacing. . . .[18]

A series of usually three periods called ellipsis is used to indicate omissions of material from a passage.[19]

Footnotes may be placed "at the bottom of the page . . . separated from the text by a horizontal line. If a line is used, it is typed a single space below the text and followed by one blank line."[20] Lesikar prefers the separation line to be one and one-half or two inches.[21] Generally, typewriting textbooks state that a two-inch line is adequate (20 pica strokes; 24 elite strokes). The line is constructed by striking the underscore key.

From a typing standpoint, reserve three lines of blank typing space per footnote at the bottom of the page.

---

17. <u>Report Writing for Business</u> (Homewood, Ill.: Richard D. Irwin, Inc., 1981), p. 187.

18. Ibid.

19. Ibid., p. 188.

20. Ruth I. Anderson et al., <u>The Administrative Secretary</u>: <u>Resource</u> (New York: McGraw-Hill Book Company, 1970), p. 391.

21. Lesikar, op. cit., p. 189.

Figure 6.1 A typewritten page with footnotes

or it may be set on the line and followed by a period and one or two spaces. The latter styling has become more popular recently and is much easier to type.

> *traditional styling*
> [7] Ibid., p. 223.

> *newer styling*
> 7. Ibid., p. 223.

Footnotes and endnotes are usually indented like a paragraph. The first line is indented and all other lines are set flush left (as shown on pages 256 and 258). Other common stylings are the flush-left and flush-and-hang stylings, in which the first line is set flush left and succeeding lines are indented. The following examples reproduce the first three footnotes on page 256. In these examples, the reference number is set on the line in the flush-left styling and is raised in the flush-and-hang styling; however, either of the positions for reference numbers may be used with any of the indention styles.

flush left

1. John E. Warriner and Francis Griffith, *English Grammar and Composition* (New York: Harcourt Brace Jovanovich, 1977), p. 208.

2. Ruth I. Anderson et al., *The Administrative Secretary: Resource* (New York: McGraw-Hill, 1970), p. 357.

3. Simone de Beauvoir, *The Second Sex*, trans. and ed. H. M. Parshley (New York: Alfred A. Knopf, 1953), p. 600.

flush and hang

[1] John E. Warriner and Francis Griffith, *English Gram-*

mar and Composition (New York: Harcourt Brace Jovanovich, 1977), p. 208.

² Ruth I. Anderson et al., *The Administrative Secretary: Resource* (New York: McGraw-Hill, 1970), p. 357.

³ Simone de Beauvoir, *The Second Sex*, trans. and ed. H. M. Parshley (New York: Alfred A. Knopf, 1953), p. 600.

In typewritten publications, the notes themselves are usually single-spaced, but double spacing is used between notes. When a manuscript is being typed prior to typesetting, however, the notes should be double-spaced, with triple spacing between the notes. In typeset material, footnotes and endnotes are usually set in type that is one or two points smaller than the text type. Extra space may or may not be placed between the notes according to individual preference.

When endnotes rather than footnotes are used, all of the notes are gathered together in a single list (as shown on page 256) either at the end of a chapter or other section or at the end of an entire work. When a book uses a single list of notes at the end of the entire work, the section is usually divided with chapter headings to show where the notes of a particular chapter begin and end. An endnote may be styled in any of the ways that a footnote is styled.

Content and Styling for First References

Both footnotes and endnotes provide full bibliographical information for a source the first time it is cited. However, in subsequent references, this information is provided in a shortened form. The following paragraphs describe the content and style used for first ref-

NOTES

1. John E. Warriner and Francis Griffith, *English Grammar and Composition* (New York: Harcourt Brace Jovanovich, 1977), p. 208.

2. Ruth I. Anderson et al., *The Administrative Secretary: Resource* (New York: McGraw-Hill, 1970), p. 357.

3. Simone de Beauvoir, *The Second Sex,* trans. and ed. H. M. Parshley (New York: Alfred A. Knopf, 1953), p. 600.

4. Martha L. Manheimer, *Style Manual: A Guide for the Preparation of Reports and Dissertations,* Books in Library and Information Science, vol. 5 (New York: Marcel Dekker, 1973), p. 14.

5. National Micrographics Association, *An Introduction to Micrographics,* rev. ed. (Silver Spring, Md.: National Micrographics Association, 1980), p. 42.

6. *Rules for Alphabetical Filing as Standardized by ARMA* (Prairie Village, Kans.: Association of Records Managers and Administrators, 1981), p. 14.

7. Peggy F. Bradbury, ed., *Transcriber's Guide to Medical Terminology* (New Hyde Park, N.Y.: Medical Examination Publishing Co., 1973), p. 446.

8. Kemp Malone, "The Phonemes of Current English," *Studies for William A. Read,* ed. Nathaniel M. Caffee and Thomas A. Kirby (Baton Rouge: Louisiana State University Press, 1940), pp. 133–165.

9. Robert Chambers, *Cyclopaedia of English Literature,* 2 vols. (New York: World Publishing House, 1875), vol. 1, p. 45.

Figure 6.2. A page of endnotes illustrating footnote and endnote style for references to books

erences. Subsequent references are discussed later in this section. Examples of the stylings described in this section are shown on pages 256 and 258. (The content and style for entries in bibliographies and lists of references are given in the section on Bibliographies and Lists of References later in this chapter.)

Books A footnote or endnote that refers to a book contains as many of the following elements as are relevant. Examples of each of the elements described below can be found in the references on page 256.

1. *Author's name* In footnotes and endnotes, the author's first name comes first and the last name after. If a book has more than three authors, the first author's name is followed by the phrase *et al.*, which is an abbreviation for the phrase *et alii* or *et aliae,* meaning "and others." (For examples of notes referring to books with multiple authors, see notes 1 and 2 on page 256.) If a publication is issued by a group or organization and no individual is mentioned on the title page, the name of the group or organization may be used in place of an author's name. In this case, the group or organization is thought of as being the corporate author. (For an example of a note describing a work with a corporate author, see note 5 on page 256.) In footnotes and endnotes, the author's name is followed by a comma.

2. *Title of the work* The title is underlined in typewritten manuscript and italicized in type. Each word of the title is capitalized except for articles and short prepositions other than the first word. When no

NOTES

1. John Heil, "Seeing is Believing," *American Philosophical Quarterly* 19 (1982): 229–239.

2. Donald K. Ourecky, "Cane and Bush Fruits," *Plants & Gardens* 27, No. 3 (Autumn 1971): pp. 13–15.

3. Xan Smiley, "Misunderstanding Africa," *Atlantic* (Sept. 1982): pp. 70–79.

4. Shiva Naipaul, "A Trinidad Childhood," *New Yorker* (17 Sept. 1984): pp. 63–64.

5. Gail Pitts, "Money Funds Holding Own," *Morning Union* [Springfield, Mass.] (Aug. 23, 1982): p. 6.

6. Jeremy C. Rosenberg, "Letters," *Advertising Age* (7 June, 1982): p. M–1.

7. M. O. Vassell, rev. of *Applied Charged Particle Optics,* ed. A. Septier, *American Scientist* 70 (1982): 229.

8. Joyce A. Velasquez, "The Format of Formal Reports," report prepared for the Southern Engineering Company, Johnson City, Miss. (May 29, 1985).

9. Clive Johnson, letter to Elizabeth O'Hara, 9 Nov. 1916, Johnson Collection, item 5298, California State Historical Society, San Marino, Calif.

Figure 6.3 Sample notes showing footnote and endnote styling for references to periodicals and unpublished sources

author's name is used in the note, the title comes first. This is commonly the styling for well-known reference books and for publications that have corporate authors but are more likely to be known by their titles. (For an example of a note in which the title comes first, see note 6 on page 256.)

3. *Portion of the book* If a reference is to one portion of a book (as an essay within a collection), the name of the portion should be included. The titles of chapters within nonfiction works by a single author are usually not part of a footnote reference. The titles of parts of books, such as short poems, short stories, and essays, are enclosed in quotation marks. (For an example of a reference to a work within a collection, see note 8 on page 256.)

4. *Editor, compiler, or translator* The name of an editor, compiler, or translator is preceded by the abbreviation *ed., comp.,* or *trans.* or some combination of them joined by *and.* The abbreviation is separated from the title that precedes it by a comma. (For examples of notes referring to a book with a translator or editor, see notes 3 and 8 on page 256.) If no author is mentioned on the title page, the name of the editor, compiler, or translator is placed first, followed by the abbreviation *ed., comp.,* or *trans.* (For an example of a note in which the editor's name comes first, see note 7 on page 256.)

5. *Name of the series* If a book is part of a series, the name of the series should be included. If the book corresponds to a specific volume in that series, the volume number is also included. The volume number is separated from the title by a comma. The name of the series is separated from the title of the volume by a comma and is capitalized as a title, although it is not underlined or italicized. (For an example of a note referring to a book that is part of a series, see note 4 on page 256.)

6. *Edition* If a work is other than the first edition, the number or the nature of the edition should be indi-

cated. (For an example of a note referring to a book that is not a first edition, see note 5 on page 256.)

7. *Volume number* If a work has more than one volume, the total number of volumes is given after the title and edition data. In addition, the number of the particular volume cited should precede the page number. In traditional footnote styling, a *vol.* or *vols.* precedes the volume number, but many authors now omit these abbreviations. (For an example of a note referring to a multivolume work, see note 9 on page 256.)

8. *Publishing data* The city of publication, the name of the publisher, and the year of publication should all be included. These items are usually placed within parentheses; a colon separates the city from the publisher's name. Names of states may be abbreviated, but not names of cities. A comma separates the publisher's name from the year of issue.

9. *Page number* The number of the page on which the quotation or information is found should be included. In traditional footnote styling, a *p.* or *pp.* precedes the page number or numbers; however, many authors now omit those abbreviation.

Periodicals A footnote or endnote referring to an article in a periodical should include all of the following information that is relevant. Examples of each of the elements described below can be found in the sample references on page 258.

1. *Author's name* The author's name is treated in the same way as described above for a reference to a

book. The names of writers of letters to a periodical and contributors of signed book reviews are treated like names of authors. (For examples of references to a letter and to a signed review, see notes 6 and 7 in the sample above.)

2. *Title of the article* The title of the article is enclosed in quotation marks. The words of the title are capitalized as in a book title. The title of the article is followed by a comma that is placed inside the quotation marks.

3. *Name of the periodical* The name of the periodical is treated in the way described above for the title of a book.

4. *Volume and number of the periodical* If a periodical uses both volume and number designations to identify an issue, both should be used. If a periodical uses some other system for identifying issues (as the month and year of issue), that system should be used. Note 1 on page 258 illustrates a reference to a periodical in which pages are numbered consecutively through a volume, and therefore only a volume number is required. Note 2 illustrates a reference to a periodical that uses a seasonal designation as well as a volume and number designation, and which paginates each issue independently of the volume. Note 3 illustrates a reference to a monthly magazine. Most monthly magazines have a volume and number designation, but they are more commonly referred to by month and year.

5. *Issue date* Periodicals variously use months, days, and years to identify issues. The date is written in whatever form the periodical uses, but the names of the months may be abbreviated.

6. *Page number* The number of the page on which the quotation or piece of information can be found is included. The varying use and omission of the abbreviation *p.* or *pp.* as described above for books hold true for references to periodicals as well. One situation in which the abbreviation is almost always dropped occurs when the reference is to a volume number and page number only. In that case, the volume number and page number are separated by a colon, and neither is identified with an abbreviation. Notes 1 and 7 on page 258 illustrate this styling.

NOTE: In making the decision of whether or not to include the abbreviation, writers and editors should keep in mind the needs of their readers. If most of the readers are well acquainted with footnote style, the abbreviation can be safely dropped. However, if a significant number of the readers of a text are unfamiliar with footnote styling, including the identifying abbreviation will help lessen the chances of confusion.

Unpublished materials A footnote referring to a work that is unpublished should include as many of the following elements as are known or are relevant. The elements described below are illustrated in notes 8 and 9 on page 258.

1. *Author's name* The author's name is treated in the same way as described above for a book.
2. *Title of the work* The title is enclosed in quotation marks and capitalized like a book title.
3. *The nature of the material* The reference should in-

clude a description of the document (as "letter" or "dissertation").

4. *Date* Include the date of the material if it is known.

5. *Folio number or other identification number* Include whatever kind of identification number is conventionally used with the material.

6. *Geographical location of the material* Include the name of the institution where the material can be found and the city where the institution is located.

Style and Content for Subsequent References

There are two systems that are currently used to refer to a source that has already been cited. One makes use of a shortened footnote styling; the other uses Latin abbreviations. Both systems are described below.

Shortened footnotes When the same source is cited repeatedly with intervening footnotes, shortened footnotes may be used as space-saving devices. The following styling is generally acceptable for most publications.

1. If the author's name occurs in the running text, it need not be repeated in footnote references to the work after the first one.

    first reference

      1. Albert H. Marckwardt, *American English* (New York: Oxford University Press, 1980), p. 94.

    repeated reference

      2. *American English,* p. 95.

2. If the author's name does not appear in the running text prior to a repeated reference, either of

the following stylings may be used. The styling of footnote 3 should be followed if more than one work by the same author is cited within the text.

> *repeated reference*
>
> 3. Marckwardt, *American English,* p. 95.
>
> *or*
>
> 4. Marckwardt, p. 95.

3. In repeated references to books by more than one author, the authors' names may be shortened. The styling of footnote 6 should be followed if more than one work by the same authors is cited within the text.

> *first reference*
>
> 5. De Witt T. Starnes and Gertrude E. Noyes, *The English Dictionary from Cawdrey to Johnson 1604–1775* (Chapel Hill: University of North Carolina Press, 1946), p. 120.
>
> *repeated reference*
>
> 6. Starnes and Noyes, *The English Dictionary from Cawdrey to Johnson 1604–1775,* p. 126.
>
> *or*
>
> 7. Starnes and Noyes, p. 126.

4. A long title may be shortened if it has already been given in full in an earlier footnote.

> 8. Starnes and Noyes, *The English Dictionary,* p. 126.

5. A shortened reference to an article in a periodical that has been cited earlier should include the author's last name; the title of the article, which can

be shortened if it is a long one, and if no similar title by the same author is being cited; and the page number.

    9. Goldman, "Warren G. Harding," p. 45.

Latin abbreviations While the simplified and shortened footnote stylings described above have gained wide currency, some writers still prefer to use the traditional Latin abbreviations *ibid., loc. cit.,* and *op. cit.* as space-savers in repeated references to sources cited earlier. Current usage indicates that these abbreviations need no longer be typed with underscoring or italicized in type; however, some writers still prefer this traditional styling. When a page reference follows one of these abbreviations, it may or may not be set off with a comma.

    10. Ibid. pp. 95–98.
       or
    11. Ibid., pp. 95–98.

These Latin abbreviations are capitalized when they appear at the beginning of a footnote or endnote, but not otherwise.

    The abbreviation *ibid.* (for *ibidem,* "in the same place") is used when the writer is referring to the work cited in the immediately preceding footnote. The abbreviation may be used several times in succession.

    first reference
    12. Simone de Beauvoir, *The Second Sex,* trans. and ed. H. M. Parshley (New York: Alfred A. Knopf, 1953), p. 600.

repeated reference (immediately following note 12)

   13. Ibid., p. 609.

repeated reference (immediately following note 13)

   14. Ibid.

When *ibid.* is used without a page number, it indicates that the same page of the same source is being cited as in the footnote immediately preceding. Thus, note 14 above cites page 609 of *The Second Sex*.

   The abbreviations *loc. cit.* (for *loco citato*, "in the place cited") and *op. cit.* (for *opere citato*, "in the work cited") may be used only in conjunction with the author's name, which may occur in the running text or at the beginning of the first reference. When the writer cites a book or periodical, its complete title should be included the first time it is referred to in a footnote. In subsequent references, *loc. cit.* or *op. cit.* with or without page numbers may be substituted for the title, depending on the type of citation.

   The difference between *loc. cit.* and *op. cit.* is that *loc. cit.* is used only when referring to the same page or pages of the same source cited earlier with footnotes intervening, while *op. cit.* is used to refer to a source cited earlier but not to the same page or pages of that source.

first reference

   15. De Witt T. Starnes and Gertrude E. Noyes, *The English Dictionary from Cawdrey to Johnson 1604–1775* (Chapel Hill: University of North Carolina Press, 1946), pp. 119–133.

repeated reference (with other footnotes intervening)

   18. Starnes and Noyes, loc. cit.

   21. Starnes and Noyes, loc. cit., p. 119.

The note without a page number indicates that pages 119–133 are being cited again.

Examples of the use of *op. cit.* are as follows:

first reference

22. Albert H. Marckwardt, *American English* (New York: Oxford University Press, 1980), p. 94.

repeated reference

24. Marckwardt, op. cit., p. 98.

The title of the work rather than the Latin abbreviation should be used if the writer is using material from more than one work by the same author.

Nonbibliographical Footnotes and Endnotes

Nonbibliographical notes provide additional information, commentary, or cross-references that the author does not want to include in the main text. They are keyed to the text in the same way as bibliographical notes. In texts in which bibliographical notes are keyed with superior numerals, nonbibliographical notes are included in the same sequence, as in the examples below. In some cases, authors will use numbered endnotes for bibliographical notes and footnotes keyed with reference marks for nonbibliographical notes; however, this system is not very common.

1. Lyon Richardson, *A History of Early American Magazines* (New York: Thomas Nelson and Sons, 1931), p. 8.

2. Total average circulation per issue of magazines reporting to the Bureau of Circulation rose from 96.8 million in 1939 to 147.8 million in 1945.

3. For a particularly compelling account of this episode, see James P. Wood, *Magazines in the United States* (New York: The Ronald Press Company, 1949), pp. 92–108.

4. Richardson, op. cit., p. 42.

5. For more details, see Appendix.

Texts that rely on parenthetical references for bibliographical notes can still include footnotes or endnotes for other notes. When a nonbibliographical note mentions the name of a book or article that is not the source of a quotation or piece of information in the text, footnote styling is used to describe the reference.

In some publications, there are certain nonbibliographical notes that are not keyed to the text with any kind of symbol. These include notes that an editor places at the beginning of each part of a collection of works by different authors and that identify each author. They also include notes that an author uses to acknowledge those who gave assistance or contributed to the writing of the work. One reason that these notes are not keyed is that the only logical place to put the reference mark (described below) or number would be following the title of the work or the name of the author (both of which are often set in a larger distinctive type style), and some editors and designers are reluctant to use footnote symbols in this position. These unnumbered notes are conventionally placed in the footnote position on the first page.

Reference Marks

In texts that have only a limited number of footnotes or endnotes, writers sometimes substitute reference marks for reference numbers. The traditional footnote reference symbols are listed below in the order in which they are usually used.

* asterisk
† dagger
‡ double dagger
§ section mark
‖ parallels
¶ paragraph mark
# number sign

The sequence of these symbols can begin anew with each page or with each chapter. If more than seven notes are needed in a sequence, the reference marks are doubled, as **, ††, etc.; however, if such a large number of footnotes is needed, reference numbers rather than reference symbols should probably be used. A common alternative to using the full set of symbols when only a few footnotes are needed is to use an asterisk for the first note, a double asterisk for the second, and so on without using the dagger or other marks. A variation on this that works for up to four footnotes in a sequence is to use the asterisk and dagger in the following order: *, **, †, ††.

Parenthetical References

Parenthetical references present very abbreviated bibliographical information (typically the name of the author, followed by a page number, but sometimes just a page number) enclosed in parentheses. They are placed in the main body of the text, and they refer readers to a fuller bibliographical description included in a list of references that is found at the end of the article, chapter, or book. A list of references is simply a bibliography, and details regarding its content and styling are presented in the section on Bibliographies and Lists of References, later in this chapter. For purposes of convenience, a sample list of references is included on page 271 and all parenthetical references in this section refer to it.

Most systems of parenthetical references are similar, but differences in details of styling do exist among the systems used by various academic disciplines and professional organizations. The examples in this section of the book are styled in accordance with the precepts of the *MLA Handbook for Writers of Research Papers,* second edition, to which readers of this book are referred for more details regarding parenthetical references. A discussion of two different parenthetical reference systems that are used in the sciences follows at the end of this section.

Placement of the Reference

Parenthetical references are placed immediately after the quotation or piece of information whose source they refer to. The sample on page 273 reproduces the text of the sample on page 253 and shows how the same text would appear using parenthetical references instead of footnotes. Note especially that sentence punctuation (that is, punctuation not associated with a quota-

List of References

Anderson, Ruth I., et al. *The Administrative Secretary: Resource.* New York: McGraw-Hill, 1970.

"Aristotle." *Webster's New Biographical Dictionary.* Springfield, Mass.: Merriam-Webster Inc., 1983.

Brushaw, Charles T., Gerald J. Alred, and Walter E. Oliu. *Handbook of Technical Writing.* 2d ed. New York: St. Martin's Press, 1982.

Chambers, Robert. *Cyclopaedia of English Literature.* 2 vols. New York: World Publishing House, 1875.

Lesikar, Raymond V. *Report Writing For Business.* Homewood, Ill.: Richard D. Irwin, Inc., 1981.

National Micrographics Association. *An Introduction to Micrographics.* Rev. ed. Silver Spring, Md.: National Micrographics Association, 1980.

Rules for Alphabetical Filing as Standardized by ARMA. Prairie Village, Kans.: Association of Record Managers and Administrators, 1981.

Figure 6.4 A sample list of references

tion) is placed after the reference. This means that periods and commas are placed outside of quotation marks and that run-in quoted sentences that end in an omission are styled with three spaced ellipsis points before the reference and a terminal period closed-up after the reference. If the final sentence of the extract quotation on page 273 had been set as a run-in quotation, it would appear as follows:

> Lesikar says, "The quoted passage is further distinguished from the report writer's work by single spacing . . ." (187).

Content and Style of Parenthetical References

The content and style are determined by two factors: (1) the style and content of the first element of the entry in the list of references to which it refers and (2) the bibliographical information that is included in the text around it.

These general principles are illustrated in the example on page 273. For instance, in the third paragraph, the parenthetical reference "(Anderson et al. 391)" is given because, in the list of references, the full reference to this source begins "Anderson, Ruth I., et al."

The way that bibliographical information in the text determines the styling of the parenthetical reference is illustrated in the first sentence of the first paragraph. The parenthetical reference "(187)" is sufficient, because it is clear that Lesikar is the author of the source that is being quoted. In the second paragraph, the full parenthetical reference "(Lesikar 188)" is required because it is not clear from the sentence who is the source of the information being provided.

Sometimes a reference is supported by citations to two separate sources; the two citations are enclosed in the same parentheses but are separated by a semicolon, as "(Lesikar 189; Anderson et al. 390)." Lengthy parenthetical references should be avoided because they interrupt the flow of text. Authors can avoid unwieldy parenthetical references by incorporating as much of the bibliographical information within the text as can be smoothly absorbed.

Matching the list of references The name in a parenthetical reference must correspond to a name that begins

According to Lesikar, if a "quoted passage is four lines or less in length, it is typed with the report text and is distinguished from the normal text by quotation marks" (187). However, a different procedure is used for longer quotations:

> But if a longer quotation (five lines or more) is used, the conventional practice is to set it in from both left and right margins (about five spaces) but without quotation marks. . . . The quoted passage is further distinguished from the report writer's work by single spacing. . . . (187)

A series of usually three periods called ellipsis is used to indicate omissions of material from a passage (Lesikar 188).

Footnotes may be placed "at the bottom of the page . . . separated from the text by a horizontal line. If a line is used, it is typed a single space below the text and followed by one blank line" (Anderson et al. 391). Lesikar prefers the separation line to be one and one-half or two inches (189). Generally, typewriting textbooks state that a two-inch line is adequate (20 pica strokes; 24 elite strokes). The line is constructed by striking the underscore key.

From a typing standpoint, reserve three lines of blank typing space per footnote at the bottom of the page.

The first line of a footnote is indented from one to six (but usually two or five) spaces from the left margin, depending on the writer's preference or the style manual being followed. The footnote may be introduced with the applicable superscript Arabic numeral, unpunctuated and separated from the first letter of the author's first name by one space; or it may be introduced by the

Figure 6.5 A typewritten page with parenthetical references.

an entry in the list of references. In general, the last name of the author is usually sufficient within a parenthetical reference, as it was in the case of the references to Lesikar's book in the sample on page 273. However, if there had been another author with the last name Lesikar in the list of references, it would have been necessary to include both first and last name, as "(Lesikar, Raymond, 188)." Alternatively, if the list of references had included two different books, both of which were by Raymond Lesikar, it would have been necessary to include both the author's name and the book's title (which may be shortened) in the parenthetical reference, as "(Lesikar, *Report Writing* 188)." The following paragraphs explain some other special cases.

1. *A work with two or three authors* The list of references on page 271 includes an entry for a book by Charles T. Brushaw, Gerald J. Alred, and Walter E. Oliu. A parenthetical reference to that work would take the following form:

    (Brushaw, Alred, and Oliu 182–184)

2. *A work with more than three authors* A work with more than three authors is listed in the list of references under the name of the first author, followed by the phrase *et al.* The reference to Anderson et al. in the third paragraph of the sample on page 273 illustrates this style.

3. *A work by a corporate author* The list of references on page 271 includes an entry in which National Micrographics Association is given as the author. A parenthetical reference to that work would also use

National Micrographics Association as its author, although the name may be abbreviated.

> (National Micrographics 42)
>
> *or*
>
> (Natl. Micrographics 42)

4. *A work listed by its title* The list of references on page 271 includes an entry for a book *Rules for Alphabetical Filing as Standardized by ARMA*. A parenthetical reference to that work should also refer to it by its title, which may be shortened for convenience.

> (*Rules for Alphabetical Filing* 14)
>
> *or*
>
> (*Rules* 14)

Locators Usually the only locator that is required in a parenthetical reference is a page number. However, sometimes additional or alternate information is needed to help the reader find the original source. The following paragraphs describe some of these special situations. Note that in all cases no punctuation separates the author's name or the title from the locator and that no abbreviation is used to identify the nature of the locator unless confusion would result from its omission (but see the note following paragraph 1 below).

1. *A multivolume work* The list of references on page 271 includes a reference to Robert Chambers's two-volume *Cyclopaedia of English Literature*. A reference to that work would have to include a volume designation as well as a page number. The volume num-

ber and the page number are separated by an unspaced colon.

(Chambers 1:45)

NOTE: If an entire volume of a multivolume work is being referred to, the abbreviation *vol.* is used to make it clear that the number is a volume number and not a page number.

(Chambers, vol. 1)

2. *A reference book* A reference to an entry in a reference book often begins with the name of the entry being cited, as in the entry for "Aristotle" on page 271. A parenthetic reference need only mention the name of the entry, as no page number is included in the list of references. The name of the reference book should be mentioned in the text preceding such a reference; otherwise, the reader must consult the list of references to know what source is being cited.

("Aristotle")

3. *Literary works* Parenthetical references to literary works often include references to stanzas, lines, verses, chapters, books, parts, and the like. This is often very useful to readers trying to find a particular passage, because they may be using an edition of the work whose pagination differs from that of the edition used by the author of the note.

References to unpublished sources Parenthetical references are also used to cite unpublished sources that are not listed in a bibliography, such as letters to the author or telephone interviews. The following information should be included: the name of the person providing the information, the type of source, and the date, as "(Paul Roberts, letter to the author, Sept. 1986)." Any of these elements may be omitted from the parenthetical reference if included in the text.

Parenthetical Reference Systems Used in the Sciences

Two other systems of parenthetical citation that are used mostly in the social and natural sciences are the author-date system (also called the name-year system) and the number system.

Author-date system In the author-date system the parenthetical reference contains the author's last name and the date of publication with no intervening punctuation. A third element, a page number, is optional. If the author's name is mentioned in the introductory text, only the date and possibly the page number are needed within the parentheses. By referring to the list of references, the reader can find complete bibliographical information about the work. However, lists of references written in connection with the author-date system must also follow the scientific styling of placing the date after the author's name in each entry.

A book or article by two or more authors would be represented by the following stylings:

> (Martin and Zim 1951)
> (Martin, Zim, and Nelson 1951)
> (Martin et al. 1951)

A corporate author name or a title may be substituted when there are no individual authors. An editor's last name may also be substituted, but the name is not followed by the abbreviation *ed*.

A page number or other number indicating a division of the work is often added to the date with a comma (a colon in some stylings) between date and page numbers. For citations to the short articles so prevalent in the scientific literature, page numbers are unnecessary, but for books, page references are certainly helpful to the reader.

> (Martin et al. 1951, 147–149) *or* (Martin et al. 1951:147–149)

Volumes are indicated by Arabic numerals. Thus, "(1.147–149)" denotes volume 1, pages 147–149.

More than one work by the same author can be readily shown with the listing of a second date that follows the first with a comma between them, as "(Martin et al. 1951, 1958)." Two or more separate citations can also be included within one parenthesis if they are separated by a semicolon.

More than one work published in the same year by the same author can be indicated by adding an *a*, *b*, or *c* to the date. The same letters should be added to the dates in the entries in the list of references.

> (Martin and Zim 1952a)

Number system In the number system, the parenthetical references consist only of numerals that are keyed to numbered entries in a list of references. Sometimes the numerals are italicized to show that they represent a title. In most variations on this system, a comma and a page number may follow the key numeral, as "(*3*,259)."

A list of references developed in connection with this system is usually arranged not in alphabetical order but in order of the first citation of each entry in the text, since this arrangement is easier for the reader who wants to locate an entry on the list. Also, the year is usually written toward the end of the entry; it does not need to appear as the second element, as it would in the author-date system. Since the list is not alphabetized, it is unnecessary to use flush-and-hang indention.

The number system is not widely used. Although it takes up less space in the text, it can be no more satisfying to the reader than the system of footnote reference numbers. Furthermore, it is difficult for the editor and author to make last-minute revisions in the text where repositioning of the numbers might be involved.

Bibliographies and Lists of References

A bibliography differs from a list of references in that it lists all of the works that a writer has found relevant in writing the text. A list of references, on the other hand, includes only those works that are specifically mentioned in the text or from which a particular quotation or piece of information was taken. In all other respects, however, bibliographies and lists of references are quite similar. They both appear at the end of an article, chapter, or book, where they list sources of information that are relevant to the text. They differ from a section of bibliographical endnotes in that their entries are arranged alphabetically (as in the sample on page 271), and they use different patterns of indention, punctuation, and capitalization, as explained in the paragraphs that follow. Bibliographies and lists of references are punctuated and capitalized in the same way, and hereafter in this chapter, references to bibliographies should be understood to be inclusive of lists of references as well.

Additional detail regarding the styling of bibliographical entries is provided in the following paragraphs. For each of the kinds of entries that are described below, two examples are given. The first example is in a style used in the humanities, which is also the style used in most general writing and the style that is familiar to most writers. The second example is in a style that is representative of the social and natural sciences.

In general, bibliographical stylings used in the sciences differ from those used in general writing in that (1) the author's first and middle names are expressed with initials only, (2) the date, which is important in scientific writings, is often placed near the beginning instead of at the end of the entry, (3) less capitalization is used, (4) titles of articles are not enclosed in quotation marks, (5) book titles are not underlined or italicized, (6) dates are usually written as day-month-year, which results in less punctuation, and (7) more abbreviations are used. In content, however, the two stylings are much the same, and both rely on periods to separate each element of the bibliographical entry.

The examples used in this section by no means exhaust the possible variations on these two basic stylings. Different combinations of the styles illustrated here, as well as other alternatives, are found in print. Several of these variations are recommended by various professional organizations and academic disciplines within the social and natural sciences. The entries in this section that illustrate scientific style are based on the style described in the *CBE Style Manual,* fifth edition, published by the Council of Biology Editors. (NOTE: Some entries in this section may differ somewhat from preferred CBE style. Writers who need to style their bibliographies in strict accordance with CBE style should consult that manual.) Similar style manuals that give details of bibliographical styling used in specialized fields within the social and natural sciences are published by professional organizations in those fields.

Books

Style and content of entries   A bibliographical entry that refers to a book includes as many of the following elements as are relevant. The order of elements listed here is the order in which they appear in entries written in the styling of the humanities. Each of these elements is illustrated in the examples that begin on page 285.

1. *Author's name*   The author's name or authors' names come first, whether the author is a single individual, or a group of individuals, or an organization. Names of coauthors are arranged in the order in which they are found on the title page. A work without an author but with an editor is styled with

the editor's name first, followed by a comma and *ed.* (see paragraph 4 below). The name of the first author is inverted so that the surname comes first and can be alphabetized. In bibliographies that follow the style of the humanities, the author's name is written as it appears on the title page. In many stylings used in the social and natural sciences, the last name and first two initials are always used, regardless of how the author's name is printed on the title page. This is the style followed in this section for examples of bibliographical entries in the social and natural sciences; however, authors should remember that some confusion can result if more than one writer in the relevant subject area has the same initials and last name. The best way to avoid this difficulty is to include first names whenever there is a chance of confusion.

In the humanities and in some stylings in the social and natural sciences, if there are more than three authors, the first author's name is followed by *et al.,* which is an abbreviation for the Latin phrase *et alii* or *et aliae,* meaning "and others." In other stylings, the names of all the authors are included.

2. *Title of the work* In the humanities, the title is underlined in typewritten manuscript and italicized in type. In the social and natural sciences, the title may follow this styling or it may be left without underlining or italicization. Capitalization is either headline-style (that is, all words are capitalized except for internal articles and prepositions) or sentence-style (that is, only the first word and proper nouns and adjectives are capitalized). In the humanities, headline-style capitalization is used; in the

social and natural sciences, both styles of capitalization are used. The titles of references in the sciences that appear as examples in this chapter are unitalicized and use sentence-style capitalization. Another difference between the two stylings is that titles in the humanities include any subtitles, whereas subtitles are often omitted in bibliographies for the sciences. Subtitles are italicized and capitalized to match the styling of the titles that precede them.

3. *Portion of the book* Some bibliography entries cite only one portion of a book, as an essay within a collection or an article within a symposium. For these entries, the name of that portion is given first as a title. It is either italicized or enclosed in quotation marks, depending on its nature, or it is left alone as in stylings for the sciences. The title of the book is given next. The titles of chapters within nonfiction works by a single author are usually not included in the entry.

4. *Editor, compiler, or translator* In entries for books that have an author, the name of an editor, compiler, or translator comes after the title and is preceded or followed by the abbreviation *ed.*, *comp.*, or *trans.* or some combination of these. If no author is listed, the name of the editor, compiler, or translator is placed first in the entry—styled like an author's name but followed by a comma and the lowercase abbreviation *ed.*, *comp.*, or *trans.*

5. *Edition* If a book is other than the first edition, the number (as "2d ed." or "1986 ed.") or other description of the edition is written after the title. If the edition is identified by a word instead of a nu-

meral, the first letter in that word is capitalized, as "Rev. ed."

6. *Volume number or number of volumes* In a bibliography entry that cites a multivolume work, the total number of volumes in that work is written before the publication information, as, for example, "9 vols." There is no need to cite the volumes actually used, since this information will be in a note or in a parenthetical reference. On the other hand, if only one volume of a multivolume work was consulted, that volume alone is listed as an entry, so that the text references need cite only page numbers, not volume numbers as well.

7. *Name of the series* If the book is part of a series, the name of the series should be included, as well as the book or volume number if the book represents a specific numbered volume in that series. The series name is not italicized.

8. *Publication data* The city of publication (with the state abbreviation if the city is not well known), the name of the publisher, and the year of publication of the particular edition used—together these form the grouping called the publication data. A colon usually follows the city name, a comma follows the name of the publisher, and a period after the date ends the bibliographical entry if the styling is that used in the humanities. In stylings used in the sciences, the date often appears after the author's name.

All of this information comes from the title page and the copyright page. If the title page lists more than one city, only the first is mentioned in the bibliography. Some books are published under a special imprint name, which is usually printed on the title page above the publisher's name. In a bibliographical entry, the imprint name is joined to the publisher's name with a hyphen, as *Golden Press-Western Publishing Co.* Short forms of publisher's names are often used in bibliographies. This usage is acceptable if consistently applied. Also the word *and* and the ampersand are equally acceptable within a publisher's name if they are used consistently.

For a multivolume work that is published over a period of several years, inclusive numbers are given for those years. The phrase *in press* is substituted for the date in works that are about to be published.

9. *Locators* Page numbers are added to book entries in a bibliography only when the entry cites a portion of a book such as a story or essay in an anthology or an article in a collection. If that portion is in a volume of a multivolume work, both volume and page number are given.

Examples The following examples illustrate how each of the elements described above is styled in a number of different situations. In each case, the first example illustrates a typical style in the humanities and general publications; the second illustrates a representative style used in the social and natural sciences.

1. *Book with a single author*

  Chapman, R. F. *The Insects.* New York: American Elsevier, 1969.

Chapman, R. F. 1969. The insects. New York: American Elsevier.

2. *Book with two or three authors*

Starnes, De Witt T., and Gertrude E. Noyes. *The English Dictionary from Cawdrey to Johnson 1604–1775.* Chapel Hill: University of North Carolina Press, 1946.

Starnes, D. T.; Noyes, G. E. 1946. The English dictionary from Cawdrey to Johnson 1604–1775. Chapel Hill: University of North Carolina Press.

3. *Book with more than three authors*

Allee, W. C., et al. *Principles of Animal Ecology.* Philadelphia: W. B. Saunders Co., 1949.

Allee, W. C.; Emerson, A. E.; Park, O.; Park, S.; Schmidt, K. D. 1949. Principles of animal ecology. Philadelphia: W. B. Saunders Co.

4. *Book with a corporate author*

National Micrographics Association. *An Introduction to Micrographics.* Rev. ed. Silver Spring, Md.: National Micrographics Association, 1980.

National Micrographics Association. 1980. An introduction to micrographics. Rev. ed. Silver Spring, Md.: National Micrographics Association.

5. *Book without an author listed*

The World Almanac & Book of Facts. New York: Newspaper Enterprises Association, Inc., 1985.

The world almanac & book of facts. 1985. New York: Newspaper Enterprises Association.

6. *Book with editor listed and no author*

> Bradbury, Peggy F., ed. *Transcriber's Guide to Medical Terminology.* New Hyde Park, N.Y.: Medical Examination Publishing Co., 1973.

> Bradbury, P. F., editor. 1973. Transcriber's guide to medical terminology. New Hyde Park, N.Y.: Medical Examination Publishing Co.

7. *Book with author and editor-translator*

> Beauvoir, Simone de. *The Second Sex.* Trans. and ed. H. M. Parshley. New York: Alfred A. Knopf, 1953.

> Beauvoir, S. 1953. The second sex. Parshley, H. M., translator and editor. New York: Alfred A. Knopf.

8. *Multivolume book*

> Farrand, John Jr., ed. *The Audubon Society Master Guide to Birding.* 3 vols. New York: Alfred A. Knopf, 1983.

> Farrand, J. Jr., editor. 1983. The Audubon Society master guide to birding. New York: Alfred A. Knopf, 3 vol.

9. *Multivolume book but only one volume consulted*

> Chambers, Robert. Vol. 1 of *Cyclopaedia of English Literature.* 2 vols. New York: World Publishing House, 1875.

> Chambers, R. 1875. Cyclopaedia of English literature. Vol. 1. New York: World Publishing House.

10. *Portion of a book*

> Malone, Kemp. "The Phonemes of Current English." *Studies for William A. Read.* Ed. Nathaniel M. Caffee

and Thomas A. Kirby. Baton Rouge: Louisiana State University Press, 1940. pp. 133–165.

Malone, K. 1940. The phonemes of current English. In: Caffee, N. M.; Kirby, T. A., eds. Studies for William A. Read. Baton Rouge: Louisiana State University Press: p. 133–165.

11. *Book in a series*

Manheimer, Martha L. *Style Manual: A Guide for the Preparation of Reports and Dissertations.* Vol. 5 of Books in Library and Information Science. New York: Marcel Dekker, 1973.

Manheimer, M. L. 1973. Style manual. New York: Marcel Dekker. (Books in library and information science; vol. 5.)

Articles in Journals or Other Periodicals

Style and Content of Entries   A bibliography entry for an article in a journal or other periodical or in a newspaper includes as many of the following elements as are relevant. Examples of each of these elements can be found in the reference samples beginning on page 291. The elements are listed here in the order in which they appear in entries styled on the humanities pattern.

1. *Author's name*   The author's name is written as it appears on the printed page and is styled in the way described above for an entry that refers to a book. Names of people who write letters to a periodical or who contribute signed reviews are treated like names of authors.

2. *Title of the article*   The title of the article is written

in full as it appears in the printed article. In most bibliography stylings used in the humanities, the title and subtitle are enclosed in quotation marks (with a period before the closing quotation mark) and capitalized headline-style. Titles of articles styled for use in the social and natural sciences tend to omit the quotation marks, use sentence-style capitalization, and omit subtitles.

3. *Name of the periodical* The name of the periodical is treated in the same way as described above for a book: underlined to indicate italics in bibliographies for the humanities, but not italicized in bibliographies for the sciences. However, unlike book titles, periodical titles are fully capitalized in bibliographies in both the humanities and the sciences. In addition, there are special principles for the styling of periodical names in both categories. One is the omission of an initial article. Whereas the initial article is included in a book title but ignored in alphabetizing, the initial article of a journal title is dropped completely. Another is the use of abbreviations for journal titles of more than one word. These abbreviations are widely used in technical writing. Each discipline has its own set of abbreviations for the journals that tend to be used in that discipline. For general writing, however, these titles are written in full for the reader's convenience, and the examples that follow show journal titles in unabbreviated form. Journal titles that begin with the words *Transactions, Proceedings,* and *Annals* are often reversed for the purpose of alphabetizing so that these words come last.

Names of newspapers are treated as they appear on the masthead, except that initial articles are omitted. Also, a place name is added in brackets after the newspaper's name if it is necessary to distinguish that particular paper.

4. *Volume and number of the periodical* This information comes after the name of the periodical and identifies the particular issue cited. An issue that is identified by both volume and number should be identified in that way in a bibliography entry, as "3(2):25–37" for volume 3, number 2, pages 25–37. If the issue is identified in some other manner, as by a full date, that method is used in the bibliography entry. Issue numbers are not commonly used, however, unless the issue is paginated independently of the volume as a whole and the number is needed to identify the issue. Examples 1 and 5 below illustrate entries for a periodical in which pages are numbered consecutively through a volume and which therefore needs only a volume number. If the volume number corresponds to a particular year, as in the examples, the year in parentheses follows the volume number—but not, of course, in the scientific stylings, where the year is placed after the author's name.

Example 2 below refers to a periodical that uses a seasonal designation in addition to a volume and number designation; the pages in this issue are numbered independently of the volume as a whole. Example 3 refers to a popular monthly magazine whose issues are commonly referred to by date rather than volume or issue number. Newspapers are always identified by date.

5. *Issue date* Periodicals issued daily, weekly, monthly,

and bimonthly are usually designated by date of issue. The date follows the unpunctuated day-month-year order (27 May 1984) rather than the punctuated month-day-year order (May 27, 1984). Names of months that are spelled with more than four letters are usually abbreviated.

6. *Page numbers* Inclusive pages for the whole article are written at the end of the entry. For newspaper entries, it may be necessary to add a section number or edition identification number as well, as "p. B6." Articles that are continued on later pages are styled thus: "38–41, 159–160." The use of the abbreviations *p.* or *pp.* in bibliographies is the same as it is in footnotes (see page 262).

Examples The following examples illustrate how each of the elements described above is styled. The first example of each group illustrates a style used in the humanities and in general publications; the second illustrates a style used in the social and natural sciences.

1. *Article in journal with continuous pagination of volume*

> Heil, John. "Seeing is Believing." *American Philosophical Quarterly* 19 (1982): 229–239.
>
> Heil, J. 1982. Seeing is believing. American Philosophical Quarterly 19:229–239.

2. *Article in journal that paginates each issue separately*

> Ourecky, Donald K. "Cane and Bush Fruits." *Plants & Gardens* 27, No. 3 (Autumn 1971): pp. 13–15.
>
> Ourecky, D. K. 1971. Cane and bush fruits. Plants & Gardens 27(3):13–15.

3. *Articles in periodicals issued by date*

> Smiley, Xan. "Misunderstanding Africa." *Atlantic,* Sept. 1982, pp. 70–79.
>
> Smiley, X. 1982. Misunderstanding Africa. Atlantic, Sept.:70–79.

> Rosenberg, Jeremy C. "Letters." *Advertising Age,* 7 June 1982, p. M–1.
>
> Rosenberg, J. C. 1982. Letters. Advertising Age, 7 June: M–1.

4. *Article in newspaper*

> Pitts, Gail. "Money Funds Holding Own." *Morning Union* [Springfield, Mass.], 23 Aug. 1982, p. 6.
>
> Pitts, G. 1982. Money funds holding own. Morning Union [Springfield, Mass.] 23 Aug.:6.

5. *Signed review*

> Vassell, M. O. Rev. of *Applied Charge Particle Optics,* ed. A. Septier. *American Scientist* 70 (1982): 229.
>
> Vassell, M. O. 1982. Rev. of A. Septier, ed., Applied charge particle optics. American Scientist 70:229.

6. *Anonymous article*

> "Education at Home: A Showdown in Texas." *Newsweek,* 25 March 1985, p. 87.
>
> Anonymous. 1985. Education at home. Newsweek 25 March:87.

Unpublished Materials

Entries for unpublished materials include as many of the following elements as are known or are relevant.

1. *Author's name* The author's name is treated in the same way as described above for a book.
2. *Title of the work* If there is an official title, it is copied as it appears on the work. It is enclosed in quotation marks and capitalized like a book title in a bibliography using a styling from the humanities. If the work has no official title, a descriptive title is used, as in example 2 below, but it is not enclosed in quotation marks.
3. *The nature of the material* The entry should include a description of the document, such as "letter to the author" or "doctoral dissertation." For works without official author or title, this element is the first part of the entry.
4. *Date* The date must be included if it is known. If the date is known but is not written on the document, it is enclosed in brackets.
5. *Name of collection and identification number* Whatever information is necessary to completely identify the document is included.
6. *Geographical location* The name of the institution and the city where the materials can be located are often listed last in this kind of entry.

Examples

1. *Unpublished report*

> Velasquez, Joyce A. "The Format of Formal Reports." Report prepared for the Southern Engineering Company. Johnson City, Miss., May 29, 1985.

> Velasquez, J. A. 1985. The format of formal reports. Report prepared for the Southern Engineering Company. 29 May. Johnson City, Miss.

2. *Letter in a collection*

> Johnson, Clive. Letter to Elizabeth O'Hara. 9 Nov.
> 1916. Johnson Collection, item 5298. California
> State Historical Society, San Marino, Calif.

> Johnson, C. 1916. Letter to Elizabeth O'Hara. 9 Nov.
> Located at California State Historical Society, San
> Marino, Calif.

Format of a Bibliography

Bibliographies are always typed beginning on a new
page. Most are alphabetically arranged and indented
flush-and-hang to set off the alphabetical sequence. Initial articles that are included in a title that begins an entry are ignored in determining the alphabetical order.
All the entries are usually listed together in a single alphabetical arrangement, whether the first word is an
author's surname or the title of an anonymous work. It
is possible to divide a bibliography into categories by
date of publication or by subject matter, but such divisions are not recommended unless the single-list form
proves unmanageable.

More than one work by an author After the first listing
of an entry by an author or group of coauthors who
have more than one work listed in the bibliography,
that person's name is replaced in succeeding, adjacent
entries by a dash. In typewritten bibliographies, the
dash is usually represented by three typed hyphens.
The author is not usually expected to type this dash or
its equivalent in hyphens; instead, the editor substitutes
the dash for the author's names as needed on the copy-
edited page. The dash is followed by a period, just as a

name would be, or by a comma and an abbreviation such as *ed.*

The dash substitutes for the author's full name (or the full names of the set of coauthors) but no more. Thus, the dash may be used only when the names are exactly the same in adjacent entries. For example, if an entry for a work by Kemp Malone is followed by an entry for a work coauthored by Malone and someone else, the second entry would be spelled out. But if Malone and his coauthor wrote more than one book together, the dash would be used to replace both names in the second reference. A work by a single author precedes a work by that author and another; and works edited by an author usually follow works written by the same person.

In the general bibliographical stylings, the various works by a single author or group of coauthors are arranged alphabetically by title. In bibliographies in the social and natural sciences, however, where the date appears after the author's name, these multiple entries are arranged by date of publication. Occasionally an author publishes more than one article during a year. In these cases, the work is identified by a letter (often italicized) that follows the year. Thus, an author's works may be listed as 1977, 1979a, 1979b, 1980, and so on.

Headings Depending on their scope as explained at the beginning of this section, bibliographies may be headed *Bibliography* or *List of References*. Writings in the sciences often list bibliographical entries under the heading *Literature Cited*. If this heading is used, then only "literature"—that is, published works—and only works actually cited can be included on the list. Unpublished works that are referred to in the text must carry information such as the author's name and the title and where the work can be located, as well as the word *unpublished*, within the text or within parentheses. To avoid having to refer to an unwieldy number of unpublished works in the text, the author or editor may head the reference list *References Cited*, which allows the inclusion of unpublished works. Works in press are usually listed under *Literature Cited* heads even though they are not yet published. In lieu of the date, the entry contains the phrase *in press*.

Annotated bibliographies Annotated bibliographies are those in which the entries are written as for a regular bibliography but are then followed by a sentence or paragraph of description. Annotated bibliographies are designed to lead the reader to the most useful works for further study. Comments may be added to all or just some of the entries. The descriptive part may be run in with the bibliographical entry, or it may be set off typographically by lines of space, indentation, italics, or smaller type.

Arabic and Roman Numerals

Name	Arabic Numeral	Roman Numeral
zero	0	
one	1	I
two	2	II
three	3	III
four	4	IV
five	5	V
six	6	VI
seven	7	VII
eight	8	VIII
nine	9	IX
ten	10	X
eleven	11	XI
twelve	12	XII
thirteen	13	XIII
fourteen	14	XIV
fifteen	15	XV
sixteen	16	XVI
seventeen	17	XVII
eighteen	18	XVIII
nineteen	19	XIX
twenty	20	XX
twenty-one	21	XXI
twenty-two	22	XXII
twenty-three	23	XXIII
twenty-four	24	XXIV
twenty-five	25	XXV
twenty-six	26	XXVI
twenty-nine	29	XXIX
thirty	30	XXX
thirty-one	31	XXXI
thirty-two	32	XXXII
forty	40	XL
forty-one	41	XLI
fifty	50	L
sixty	60	LX

Name	Arabic Numeral	Roman Numeral
seventy	70	LXX
eighty	80	LXXX
ninety	90	XC
one hundred	100	C
one hundred one	101	CI
or one hundred and one		
one hundred two	102	CII
or one hundred and two		
two hundred	200	CC
three hundred	300	CCC
four hundred	400	CD
five hundred	500	D
six hundred	600	DC
seven hundred	700	DCC
eight hundred	800	DCCC
nine hundred	900	CM
one thousand	1,000	M
two thousand	2,000	$\overline{\text{MM}}$
five thousand	5,000	$\overline{\text{V}}$
ten thousand	10,000	$\overline{\text{X}}$
one hundred thousand	100,000	$\overline{\text{C}}$
one million	1,000,000	$\overline{\text{M}}$

Proofreaders' Marks

ℬ or ϒ or ℐ delete; take it out

⌒ close up; print as o ne word

ℬ delete and close up

∧ or ˃ or ⌃ caret; insert here ⟨something⟩

\# insert a space

eg# space evenly where indicated

stet let marked text stand as set

tr transpose; change order the

/ used to separate two or more marks and often as a concluding stroke at the end of an insertion

⌊ ⌊ set farther to the left

⌉ set⌉ farther to the right

⌒ set æ or fl as ligatures æ or fl

= straighten alignment

‖ ‖ straighten or align

✗ imperfect or broken character

◻ indent or insert em quad space

ℙ begin a new paragraph

ⓢⓟ spell out ⟨set 5 lbs. as five pounds⟩

cap set in capitals ⟨CAPITALS⟩

sm cap or *s.c.*	set in <u>small capitals</u> ⟨SMALL CAPITALS⟩
lc	set in ~~L~~owercase ⟨lowercase⟩
ital	set in <u>italic</u> ⟨*italic*⟩
rom	set in <u>*roman*</u> ⟨roman⟩
bf	set in <u>boldface</u> ⟨**boldface**⟩
= or -/ or ‿ or /H/	hyphen
$\frac{1}{N}$ or *en* or /N/	en dash ⟨1965–72⟩
$\frac{1}{M}$ or *em* or /M/	em — or long — dash
∨	superscript or superior ⟨^{2} as in πr^2⟩
∧	subscript or inferior ⟨$_2$ as in H_2O⟩
⌄̂ or ⋎	centered ⟨ ⊙ for a centered dot in $p \cdot q$⟩
⸲	comma
⸴	apostrophe
⊙	period
; or ;/	semicolon
: or ⊙:	colon
❝ ❞ or ⌄⌄	quotation marks
(/)	parentheses
[/]	brackets
ok/?	query to author: has this been set as intended?

Index